Faith 911

The inspiring true story of second chances

G.L. Woods

Faith 911: The inspiring true story of second chances

978-0-9855984-0-2
Copyright © 2012 by G.L. Woods
All rights reserved.

Unless otherwise identified, all Scripture quotations are taken from the *Holy Bible, New International Version* © 1973, 1978 by the International Bible Society. Used by permission.

NKJ Scriptures are taken from the *New King James Version*. Copyright © 1979, 1980, 1982 by Thomas Nelson, Inc. Used by permission. All rights reserved.

AMP Scripture quotations taken from the Amplified® Bible, Copyright © 1954, 1958, 1962, 1964, 1965, 1987 by The Lockman Foundation. Used by permission. (www.Lockman.org)

Produced and packaged by:

Vision Communications Creative and Publishing Services, Inc.
4915 Rattlesnake Hammock Road #123, Naples, Florida 34113
www.visionbookproducers.com

Managing editor: Stacie Jennings

   Graphic design: Jeff Behymer/BeGraphic

   Cover design: Jaymes Schrock/Scribbles & Scribes

Printed by: Bookmasters/www.bookmasters.com

Table of Contents

Dedication

It's been said that no one on this earth holds a crystal ball, and I believe it's by design that tomorrow is supposed to be a mystery. No family could ever be fully prepared for the kind of tragedy our family has endured. However, one thing is certain, when those tough times arose, we conquered them together as one unit.

I feel so incredibly blessed that God has given us to each other. Having a family like ours to be able to survive life's storms and cheer life's successes together is more that any man deserves.

As I dedicate this book to my wonderful wife Tina, and my twins, Bailey & Bryce, I pray that you three never forget how much I love you and that you mean everything to me!

Acknowledgements

It's never easy to step out of one's comfort zone, yet I knew that tackling such a huge undertaking of writing a book would require me to do just that. As I felt the calling to take the thoughts that were in my mind and somehow relate them to paper, the natural human emotions of fear, nervousness, and doubt set in.

From the very beginning one person enthusiastically supported this mission—my mother. She never even gave me the opportunity to ask for her help; she volunteered first. Even though hundreds of miles now separate us, we've been connected at the heart from the time I was born.

Without her immeasurable dedication and willingness to contribute both her skill and time to the development of this story, *Faith 911* would never have come to reality. I truly believe with all my heart that there are just two people in the world who could have accurately captured this powerful story, my mother, Joan, and I.

Words could never come close to describing the gratitude I feel towards her, so I'll only say, "Mom, I love you."

Your son,
G.L.

Foreword

Love, joy, peace, forthright, and enthusiastic are words I think of when I think of G.L. Woods. I've known him some 25 years and every year that I know him, I have a greater appreciation for what he stands for. In my lifetime, I have learned that people are the most important blessings that have ever been put into one's life.

When God created all things, He made them good; but when He created people, He made them special and above all other creatures. People have been a great blessing to me, but some of the people have helped me to make my life what it is today. G.L. Woods is one of those people. He is certainly the cream that comes to the top. He is a great salesman, but most importantly, he's a great man, a great husband, and a great dad.

The truth of who he is came out several years ago when he had his motorcycle accident and was injured to such an extent that the doctors gave him little hope. During this period, instead of giving up, G.L. totally turned to God and found the strength to defy all the odds, and to recover to the extent that he lives a very normal life. Many men would have given up in total despair, but not G.L. Because of his faith in God and the inner strength that was given to him in the inner man, he is now a blessing to everyone he meets, and he has a great testimony to the glory of God. He certainly has been a tremendous blessing to me and to Ozark National Life Insurance Company.

G.L. has great perseverance and integrity, something that the world is short of. I am sure that his greatest years are ahead of him as he shares his testimony with so many who need to know about his strength and whence it comes.

I am delighted that G.L. would take time to write a book and share his story with the world. It shows what a man can do when he puts his trust in the Creator.

Charles N. Sharpe

Chairman of the Board and President,
Ozark National Life Insurance

Founder and President,
CNS International Ministries, Inc.

1

If I Could Turn Back Time

Is it possible for time to actually stand still? Maybe not, but ask any accident victim—someone who's experienced the horror of barreling inescapably towards impact—and they'll tell you without a doubt that time does, indeed, unmercifully, slow down.

As I tumbled across the rain-soaked West Virginia mountainside that October afternoon, everything seemed to be happening in slow motion. I recognized my boots and gloves as they repeatedly passed the field of vision through my motocross helmet, but whose lifeless rag-doll arms and legs were wearing them? I felt as if someone had cut off my head, and that it was bouncing wildly out of control. Pine trees, patches of gray sky, and soggy heaps of fallen leaves appeared to be performing a bizarre flash dance before my eyes, while all I could think was *My God! My God! What have I done?*

When my body finally came to a stop, I was lying flat on my back, gasping for air. Because of my hard riding style, I'd crashed my motorcycle and knocked the wind out of myself lots of times before. But this was different. My entire body felt like it was made of cement, and I couldn't believe how hard it was to breathe. I panicked.

1

Why is my body so heavy?

Why won't it move?

Why can't I get up?

That's when I realized that I hadn't knocked the wind out of myself at all; I was totally paralyzed from my neck down. I had just become a quadriplegic.

Everyone's heard someone describe a near-death experience as their life flashing before their eyes. I'd never understood exactly what that meant until now, as I began to visualize what my own life had consisted of. It was like an edited newsreel of all of the milestones being played through my mind at hyper-speed.

In the small East-Central Missouri farming community that I grew up in was a sleepy little town where neighbors watched out for neighbors and kids could safely be kids, doing all the crazy things only they can dream up. Jonesburg, Missouri, was an incredible place to live as a kid, because during the 1970s there was none of the hustle and bustle of the big city. Jonesburg had a population then of a whopping 450 people; today there are barely 900. Even the largest town in our county back in the mid-70s only had 2200 people. We had no idea how good we had it: a simple life with no concerns or complications.

My kid brother, John, wasn't born until 1974, so for the first ten years of my life I was an only child, which meant I was used to finding ways to entertain myself. Summertime was the best, jumping out of bed early to meet friends at the ball diamond. We didn't usually have enough kids to play two full teams against each other, so we would just play 500 all day (a batting and fielding game). Even the girls who were tomboys would play. Truth be known, a couple of the girls were better ball players than I was, but it was all good because we were just a bunch of pals hanging out.

I was never a great athlete at any one particular sport. I enjoyed trying them all, but I struggled to find my niche. Of the mainstream sports, I probably liked football the best. Growing up during the ongoing Super Bowl rivalry of the 1970s between the Dallas Cowboys and the Pittsburg Steelers made me love the game even more. However, my size and weight hindered me from playing, so I would find myself warming the bench on second or third string. It was discouraging because I wanted to see action. Maybe that's why I found myself drawn to more extreme sports, sports that didn't require rounding up a team of kids. Sports that I could enjoy anytime I wanted. The only person I needed to show up was me.

During that time of my life, my heroes were Muhammad Ali, Evil Knievel, and world champion motocross racer Bob "Hurricane" Hanna. Like a lot of kids during the 70s, my friends and I would try to duplicate jumps on our bicycles that we'd seen Evil Knievel do on his motorcycle. We'd do jumps over willing neighborhood kids, their bicycles, and any other stack of stuff we could find. The thrill I felt after accomplishing each feat made me hunger for the next challenge. After a while, even the most recent accomplishment just wasn't enough. Nothing ever seemed to be enough. I always needed more: longer jumps, higher jumps, and faster speed. I was a speed junky from day one, needing a fix, whatever it took to satisfy my need for an adrenalin rush.

The kids I hung out with were just like me, wanting that rush in life, afraid of nothing, certainly not afraid of getting hurt. We soon graduated to adding rows of trash cans to our bicycle jumps. One day that thrill subsided. A kid yelled, "Hey, I've got a *great* idea! Let's first set the trash cans on fire!"

We added large amounts of gasoline to make sure the flames would be seen from outer space. I was the first to go, and I sped toward the jump ramp with all my might. Just as I became airborne, my friends lit the gas and I felt the whoosh from the explosion. It looked like a scene from Hiroshima in WWII as my bike and I sailed through the fireball, landing safely on the other side. My friends were ecstatic as we all screamed, dancing around and high-fiving each other, until one of them said, "What's that smell?" My first fiery try had singed all the hair off my arms and legs. I hope as my mother reads this, she doesn't have a heart attack (sorry, Mom).

From then on, "Airtime" was the name of the game. I was always looking for any opportunity to get my bike off the ground. I knew all the best places in town for good air: raised sidewalks, loading docks, gravel or dirt piles—anything high enough to provide a jump site.

One day I was flying at top speed toward one of the best jumps I knew, a buckled sidewalk down the street from my house. I was certain that this would be my personal best record long jump; I would be king of the heap. But instead of being king of the heap, I ended up *in* a heap. I was going so fast that when I went airborne off that buckled concrete I hit a telephone pole in mid-air and knocked myself unconscious. This was my first real insight into the notion that "Airtime" could be painful. More than thirty-five years later, the chunk I took out of that pole is still visible. Everyone wants to leave a mark in this world, but I didn't intend mine to be like that.

During that time I also became interested in skateboarding, a new thrill I hadn't conquered. I would practice for hours in our driveway to perfect my riding skills. It didn't take long for me to become bored with just riding up and down the drive. I would spend hours seeing how many 360-degree spins I could do or how far I could ride a wheelie. I soon graduated to jumps and ramps. I sometimes begged my mom to take me to the city, about an hour away, where there was a real skateboard park complete with deep bowls and half pipes. It was there that I first witnessed a kid ride his board standing on his hands. I thought to myself, *a handstand—are you kidding me?* It was hard enough to ride on my feet, but I was awe-struck with what I had just seen. I knew I had to learn how to do it.

I recruited a couple of friends to hold my feet in the air while I learned over a period of several months to balance on the board upside down. This was a painful experience as I skinned my knees, my elbows, and especially my head. But once I mastered this skill, I rode more on my hands than on my feet.

During that same time, my dad introduced me to the world of motorcycles. An avid rider himself, he owned a '74 Suzuki TS125 and he taught me how to ride his bike in our pasture. Since I was only 12 years old, my legs weren't yet long enough to be on the bike and still touch the ground. My dad set up two parallel hay bales in the field where I rode, with enough space for me to ride between them and stop so I could get on and off. This worked great unless I crashed or killed the engine out in the pasture, then I would have to push the bike to the nearest tree or fence post to use as a prop so I could climb back on.

Bicycles were now a thing of the past. This motorcycle was real power. Now I could go faster than ever before and make jumps farther then my legs could propel me. Evil Knievel, watch out, there's a new sheriff in town and he's not afraid of *anything*.

About this same time Dad asked me, "Would you like to buy a motorcycle of your own?" Are you kidding? Would I? He had accumulated some silver coins with my savings account money, and with a recent surge in silver prices, what had been about $100 in face value was now worth around $500. It was just enough to get a decent, used 1973 Suzuki TC 125 Enduro (dirt/street) bike and a helmet. Some of the kids I knew rode without a "skid lid," but I never mounted up without my helmet on. I knew I would be riding hard and fast, and that it would just be a matter of time before that helmet might be needed.

At age 12, I thought that motorcycle was the coolest thing ever.

5

Of course my dad was horrified when the first thing I did was remove anything that resembled a street legal bike including the headlights, taillights, and chrome trim. I mean, you can't be a real motocross rider if your bike has chrome, right?

My folks couldn't keep me off that thing. During school I couldn't think about anything else but getting home and riding my dirt bike. As soon as I walked through the door, I dropped my books, grabbed a snack, scurried to the garage to my bike, and headed for the small pasture behind our house where I rode daily.

Like most kids, the more I rode, the braver I became. As I learned my limitations, I always seemed to ride right up to that edge. What was the sense of riding if you weren't going to push it to the limit? I totally thrashed that bike for two years, day in and day out. I lost count of how many sets of handlebars I mangled and how many fenders I broke off. I laughed to myself when I eventually sold that bike to my band teacher, who I really didn't like much anyway, because I knew what I had put that bike through. If motorcycles could talk, I'm sure mine would have been saying, "Thank you. Thank you for saving me from that little monster."

After honing my rookie skills on that first bike, I was ready for the big league. I purchased a *real* motocross bike, a 1978 Suzuki RM 125. Finally, this was the real deal race bike. Coming off that docile enduro, this new one felt like an animal. I was a bit intimidated at first, but I shook off the feeling after a few days. I couldn't believe how fast that thing was. When I revved the RPMs into the power band, it seemed like it could actually jump out from under me. And I *loved* it. By this time my younger brother, John, was nearly five, and my dad put him on a little 50cc Suzuki bike. It was time for him to join the fun; this was a family affair.

In no time John became a very good rider as well. Like most teenagers, there were days that I didn't feel like having my baby brother tagging along on my rides. I'd try to discourage him by coaxing him over on his little JR 50 to a big mud hole, and me on my 125, I'd let the rear tire eat mud. That poor kid would be covered from head to toe with slime from the rooster tail I was throwing. He'd run to the house to tell on me, and I'd usually get grounded from riding for a few days. But all in all, I generally considered the punishment worth it.

On the opposite end of town there was a kid a little younger than me who actually had a racetrack at his house. I couldn't afford to be caught riding a dirt bike that wasn't street legal, not to mention I wasn't even old enough to have a driver's license. I would push that bike, with all my gear on, nearly a mile through town just to ride with him. At times I would get so tired of pushing it that I'd take a chance, fire it up, and ride through the alleys. After the town marshal stopped me several times and threatened to impound my bike, I figured it wasn't worth losing my ride.

My friends and I rode every kind of terrain we could find: MX tracks, hill climbs, creeks, quarries, you name it. As I said earlier, I was never really able to find my niche in the school sports scene, but now I had finally found something at which I could excel. Suddenly, the playing field was even. I didn't have to be a certain size or have a particular athletic skill. The biggest advantage here was having guts. During all the years I rode, I remember one thing the most: I was never afraid of anything (almost to a fault). I laugh now when I see the bumper stickers on the back of some kid's vehicle that reads "No Fear," and I think to myself, *I could have been a poster child for that phrase.*

I joke sometimes that I was a drug baby, meaning my mother *drug* me to church as far back as I can remember. Early on, it was my mother and I who would attend church. My dad went some, but his attendance was inconsistent, though I always remember seeing him pray every night in bed before going to sleep. On more than one occasion, he made the comment that you don't have to go to church to go to heaven. Even though those words had a profound impact on me, I was baptized into Christ at age 12.

I know baptism is meant to be a life-altering event, a cleansing of sin and a renewing of life. However, at that age it just didn't have the meaning for me that it should have, probably because of my lack of emotional and spiritual maturity. I didn't take the ramifications of it nearly as serious as I should have. Baptism didn't change my life like I thought it would.

I learned some major life lessons growing up where I did. I was blessed to have wonderful parents, Gary and Joan Woods, who had great integrity and a solid work ethic. Work always came before play. It was this early mindset that I have carried with me all my life. As soon as I was old enough to push a lawn mower, I built a customer base during the summer. While most of my friends were still playing their days away, it was *cha-ching* time for me.

When winter came, snow days from school meant dollar days for me. I would wake up as early as possible and head out with my snow shovel, clearing sidewalks and driveways throughout town. I had to make an early start if I wanted to make any real money. Making the mistake of sleeping in could be expensive because a few of the older boys in town would have the good stops already shoveled. Of course I could always count on the crazy old man who lived down on Main Street. He paid the older boys to shovel snow off his car, and then when I came along he would pay me to shovel it back on again. Go figure.

When I was 14 I landed a real job at the local grocery store, stocking shelves and bagging groceries. For the first time in my life I was being paid an hourly wage and punching a time clock. It was this financial windfall that helped to fund my riding addiction. At that age it was difficult to afford any fancy engine machine work to increase the speed of my bike, so my buddies and I would perform the redneck engine hop-up to all our dirt bikes. We figured out that by eliminating the 1/8-inch thick metal head gasket from the top of the motor, we could really increase the compression, thus increasing the performance. Our redneck customization wasn't too great on the life of a motor, but man, did it run. If my dad had known we were doing that, he would've had a cow.

As time went on, our pasture became a motocross track, complete with jumps. We even built a jump directly over the top of the livestock watering pond. Some of my buddies wouldn't even consider attempting it because it was a jump they certainly didn't want to come up short on. But not knowing for sure if we were going to clear it was such a rush that, for me, it was worth the risk.

Late that same year I entered my first motocross race in the novice 125 class, and the adrenalin rush was indescribable. My dad also raced that night in what we referred to as the old man's class. I laugh now, because it actually was the age 35-plus class, hardly old. Of course, when you're only 14, age 35 seems ancient. Watching Dad ride in that race made me *very* nervous. I was never afraid when I was the one doing the riding, yet I was terrified that he'd get hurt. That's when I realized what he must be feeling when I was out there. I wondered then if he wished he had never introduced me to the sport, not that it would have made much difference, because I have no doubt I would have eventually found it on my own.

A lot of the riding crew I hung out with was older than me. At the time I thought I was cool, hanging out with the older guys, but in retrospect, I was living life way beyond my young years. At that age, it was hard for me to hold my ground because I wanted so badly to fit in with the crowd—and that crowd was running hard and fast. I sure didn't want to be left behind. It was an education I wasn't prepared for so soon. I can vividly remember my first time watching one of the older guys ride. His reputation for crazy stunts was legendary. I couldn't believe what I was seeing, the risks he was willing to take. His fearlessness actually made me cringe, but at the same time I was awestruck. In the back of my mind I wanted that to be me someday.

More and more of my time was spent with these older boys, both on and off my bike, and drinking alcohol was part of their lifestyle. When you live in such a small community, it's easy to know where to buy beer when you're under age. Looking back, I know now that God must have had His protective bubble around us naïve kids because we were certainly making *no* effort to shield ourselves from anything detrimental to our health and well-being.

There was one small, isolated gas station and convenience store north of the interstate, and the owner would regularly hire me to climb to the top of his sign to change the price of gas. Since the sign needed to be visible from the interstate, it sat atop a 100-foot tower. The owner was scared to climb the tower himself, so when he called I would just ride my bicycle down there, scale that tower, and change the numbers. It was a quick 15- to 20-minute job, and for this he would gladly pay $20; easy money for me. My immunity to fear had just become my golden cow. Of course, I kept my new career a secret from my parents because I knew they would kill my cow. Because of this business relationship, the store would eventually become my main beer supplier when I turned 16. The owner was my beer daddy, so to speak.

Once I was old enough to drive, I really got turned loose into the world. However, I didn't handle it too well. Without being spiritually grounded, I began to run even harder with the crowd. Between the ages of 16 and 18, I attended at least one keg party every week, sometimes my own. I was a good student in high school and somehow I'd always make it on the honor roll. But when the weekend came, look out, it was party time.

Throughout my junior and senior years in high school, it wasn't uncommon to tell my folks that I wanted to have a few friends over for a small poker game while they were out of town. These small gatherings invariably turned into full blown two-keg parties. When word spread around the county that there was a party at the Woods' house, the kids came pouring in. One night the house was so jammed full of party animals that you could hardly find your way through. As luck would have it, Mom and Dad arrived home a day earlier than planned. Imagine my shock. Talk about *bad* timing. There were so many cars in our driveway, not to mention up and down the street, that my folks had to park a block away. This gave Mom and Dad plenty of time to build up a full head of steam by the time they burst through the door.

I was in the basement playing poker when suddenly everything went unnaturally quiet. I only had time to glance up before I saw my dad's searing eyes staring at me over the crowd. My heart began to pound. He didn't say a word. He just held up two fingers and I immediately understood what that meant: you've got two minutes to clear out.

It was as if the cops had arrived; kids started scrambling, heading for all available exits. When Mom walked into the kitchen, her shoes actually stuck to the beer-splattered floor like she was walking through some cheap bar. Busted! I learned that night my dad was not a violent person. Otherwise I would not have lived to see another day.

Like my friends, my need for speed had spilled over from bicycles, to dirt bikes, and now to my car. Montgomery County had several roads that were ideal for drag racing, and that is where we would all meet on Friday and Saturday nights to line 'em up. We learned early on never to return to the scene of the crime two nights in a row. If we drag raced at one place on Friday night, the cops would be waiting there Saturday night. But we would be at another stretch of road across the county. Inevitably, someone would show up with a keg of beer in the bed of their truck and it was capital P: party time!

We just assumed that a keg of beer and drag racing went hand-in-hand; you couldn't have one without the other. What a stupid idea, but then, teenagers believe they are indestructible. Besides, drinking and drag racing was cool. Those two things are dangerous enough by themselves, but combined they can be lethal. I cringe today at the thought of what could have happened. Of course we heard about things going bad in other places—horrific crashes and even deaths—but it was always to someone else. Fortunately it never happened to us.

I don't doubt that God was protecting me from my own stupidity.

Bottom Row - S. Jaspering, T. Van Doren, G. Woods, C. Adams, J. Boone, L. Johnson, D. Brookman, K. Rakers, M. O'Reilly, S. Hoover Mgr., 2nd Row - K. Knudson Mgr., J. Arens, T. O'Keefe, S. Gotsch, T. Kozemski, J. Wyatt, D. Eldringhoff, B. Borchelt, P. Waldron, B. Ross Mgr., J. Reynolds Mgr., 3rd Row - B. Schneider Asst. Coach, D. Magruder, K. Winford, M. Bishop, C. Powell, D. Logan, D. Hillebrand, W. Fry, C. Shoemaker, A. Brake Head Coach, 4th Row - D. Edwards, D. Oliver, M. Thurman, K. Worland, B. Holden, J. Futhey, J. Cavender, D. Owens

13

2
Welcome to the Real World

My first serious motocross crash happened just one month after I graduated from high school in May of 1983. Of course, I'd had hundreds of minor spills up to that point, but nothing that couldn't be cured with a cast or a few stitches. Anyway, I thought that crashes were just part of riding, the price you had to pay to play.

During a pre-race practice lap I came up short when I tried to land a double jump, and before I knew what happened my bike and I were headed for disaster. A friend who witnessed the crash later described it like this: "You flew through the air upside-down with your feet still on the pegs, your hands still gripping the handlebars, and your rear-end plastered to the seat, just like you were still riding, but upside down."

Within a millisecond I was pile-driven into the dirt. I landed on my back with my bike on top of me. I was knocked unconscious, and when I finally came to, the first thing I saw was a group of concerned faces hovering above me. Although my back was killing me, people helped me up and walked me off the track. Someone called an ambulance as a precaution, and I was propped up against a tree while we waited for it to arrive. I knew something wasn't right. I was having pain like I'd never experienced before, but I didn't know what the problem was.

Since it was Sunday, the ambulance took me directly to a local doctor's home-office. He came out to the ambulance and poked around on me for a few minutes, then he said, "I think he's fine, but you might take him on to the hospital to have him checked out."

What followed was a grueling 25-mile drive, and my back felt every rough spot in the road. When I got to the hospital, I was surprised at the level of concern expressed by the ER staff as they frantically rushed me through a series of X-rays and scans. Finally, a doctor came in to let me know that my parents were on their way. "Am I staying?" I asked.

"Oooh yeah," he said with finality. He went on to explain that I had broken my back in four places and they were concerned about damage to my pancreas. He made it perfectly clear that I had dodged a bullet because I was still able to move my legs and feet. The worst part of the injury was a hairline crack completely across one vertebra. If it shifted, I could sever my spinal cord and be paralyzed from the waist down.

Someone had just slammed the brakes on my life. I'm sure that my face went white when I realized the severity of my injury. After all, I had been hauled up off the ground at the track and transported with no real effort to protect my back. I'm sure my friends thought I'd just rung my bell. It was not the first time they'd seen this happen. I was 18; I had just graduated from high school and I was ready to take on the world, but not from a hospital bed.

I had never seen my folks so serious as when they walked into my hospital room. It must have scared them to death. Years ago, my dad's old army buddy had been paralyzed from the neck down in a car crash at age 35, and he was now confined to a nursing home. I know Dad was terrified of that happening to me. Clearly, recovery was going to take a very long time.

Later, as I was lying in my hospital bed feeling sorry for myself, an old guy came to visit the man who shared my room. The visitor politely asked me what had happened. Not really feeling talkative, I mumbled, "A dirt bike accident."

"Was it your bike?" he asked.

"Yeah."

"Did you buy it?"

I was getting a little irritated. "Yes," I said.

"Well, for Pete's sake kid, why did you buy one when you could go to any funeral home and get one for free?"

I wasn't in any mood for a smart-aleck remark as I thought to myself, "The old coot, what does he know?"

Things are much different today, but at that time treatment for my kind of injury didn't include surgery, pins, screws, or rods. Instead, time was to be my healer. After a few days in the hospital, it was determined that I would eventually be put into a body cast. But first, I would be sent home for one month to allow the fractured vertebrae and bones to mend. The doctor was adamant about me lying perfectly still, flat on my back, for the entire month.

I was sent home by ambulance to an awaiting hospital bed that had been set up in our living room. The driver did his very best to smooth out the road during the long two-hour trip home. In spite of his efforts, I felt every slight imperfection in the pavement, which caused excruciating pain. I was glad to be home, but exhausted from the trip. I knew that in four weeks I would again be facing that two-hour ambulance trip back to the hospital for my body cast. Yuk!

I'm sure some people would think that staying in bed for a solid month would be kind of cool, but I'm here to say...*wrong!* Imagine having to lie flat on your back 24/7, unable even to roll onto your side without someone to turn you. All I could see from the bed was the visual half of the living room that was directly in front of me. I stared up at the ceiling, studying every flaw.

Having graduated from high school, I was supposed to be on my own, independent and free. Now here I was, totally dependent on my folks, or an in-home nurse, to provide for my every need. The TV had been raised off the floor high enough for me to see it from my hospital bed. With nothing else to do and certainly nowhere to go, I spent hours on end playing Atari video games. My friends coming to visit inevitably made the mistake of challenging me to a game or two. After having had plenty of time to perfect my gaming skills, I generally beat them unmercifully.

I tolerated my friends filling me in on their active lives, what they were doing, who they saw, what latest killer party they went to… blah, blah, blah! How was I going to compete with that when my life revolved around bedpans, urinals, sponge baths, and eating while lying flat on my back?

That month spent confined to a bed felt like a year, an eternity in an 18-year-old's life. A calendar hung by my bed and the days were crossed off as I counted down the time for my return to the hospital. I don't believe I'd thought the body cast part of the plan all the way through. All I was thinking was I wouldn't be stuck in bed anymore. On the day that the ambulance arrived to take me back to the hospital, I knew that I would soon be back in action, no longer MIA from the social scene. I was about to find out differently.

The reality of a body cast immediately set in and I was shocked to see how big it was, running from my armpits down to my groin, encasing my entire torso. My muscles were already weak from a month of lying inactive, and the thick plaster cast, which weighed more than 25 pounds, didn't help matters. But even though I would be in that uncomfortable, itchy cast for the next two months, at least I was free.

Try to imagine spending July and August in a plaster body cast during any normal summer. This was the summer of 1983, one of Missouri's hottest on record. Not the best summer to be stuck in a plaster cast—*wow*! As soon as I returned home, I hopped in my car, ready to jump-start my life again. Immediately I picked up where I had left off before the accident, rejoining the teenage party scene, which was in full pre-college swing. We were headed for college and I knew that it might be a long time before I saw some of these kids again. I was easy to spot in a crowd wearing my bib overalls, because blue jeans wouldn't button around my cast. My fashion statement was Farmer in the Dell meets Motocross Racer. I had no intention of wasting valuable time nursing a hurt back; I needed action.

One day, while my folks were at work, I decided to see if I could just sit on my motorcycle with that bulky cast around my torso. I found out that I could. Then I wondered if I could kick start it; surely it wouldn't hurt to take a quick spin in the yard. To my excitement, the motorcycle started. Since I was in the yard already I figured that I might as well go out into the pasture, even though I was concerned the neighbors might rat me out to the folks and that would be *bad*. After spending that month of misery confined to a hospital bed, common sense should have screamed, "Don't get back on that bike!" But it didn't—so I did.

At the time, I didn't realize I was addicted to the adrenaline rush that came from my insatiable desire for speed. I shared the same view of my addiction as the view held by any other addict: everyone else is wrong and nothing is gonna happen to me. I couldn't comprehend everyone else's fear and concern for me; I just wanted to ride again. It was kind of like the old saying that goes "Get back on the horse that bucked you."

Looking back, I wish I had been scared enough to be at least a little cautious. I was so naïve that I thought I had just made it through the worst storm I'd ever have to face—but my folks saw it differently. From that point on my kid brother wasn't allowed to ever ride his Suzuki again. At 8 years of age, his riding career was over, thanks to me.

>>>>>>>>>>>>>>>>>>>>>>>>>>>>>>>

I was still in the body cast when I started college in the fall of 1983. I was working part-time at a bank near the campus, trying to juggle my three lives: work, study, and social. I was in major party mode. I joke about it today, telling people that when I was in school I majored in "wild-life."

It was late September when my body cast was cut off, and I was surprised when my doctor commented on how well my injury had healed. But the shocker was when he said he'd release me to finish out the racing season if I wanted to. I was expecting more cautionary advice from a medical professional, but I must admit, he was my kind of guy.

I had always been a good student in high school, but like many college freshmen, I wasn't sure what I wanted to do with my life. Even without the confines of a body cast, I just couldn't seem to settle into the campus scene. I've never considered myself a quitter, which made the decision I was about to make embarrassing. I dropped out of college after only one semester, disappointing my parents terribly.

I realized that I had no real direction for my life, now that I had left college. I'd never had a problem finding a job because I was always a hard worker. Even during my high school years, I worked two or three jobs at any given time. My folks told me something when I was a kid that had stuck with me: if a man is willing to pay you for work, give him his money's worth.

When I was 19, I was given the opportunity to buy my dad's business, a produce distribution route. I would be responsible for supplying the grocery stores, schools, and restaurants in a two county area. All of a sudden, I was an owner-operator of my own company and I had people depending on me. Even though I was still a kid, I had to learn to deal with adults on their level. Although I was still trying to find my niche at that time in my life, my business was successful and I ran it responsibly during the week.

Things were going well and I was making more money than I ever had before. My job responsibilities, however, were a far cry from my wild weekend life where I was still throwing caution to the wind and living my life the way I wanted to live it.

I had moved out of my parents' home and was renting a small house in Jonesburg. Let the games begin! I no longer worried about Dad killing my parties with his "you've got two-minutes" drill. My life was a dangerous combination of no strings attached, a lot of immaturity, and cash in my pocket. I made my own rules and was free to live life as I saw fit. I was in control of my life, and that's just the way I liked it.

During that time, I also became seriously involved in physical fitness. I became a gym rat. I lifted weights every day and studied Tae Kwon Do in order to earn my black belt. After all, the movie *Karate Kid* was all the rage, and I was hungry to learn. Plus, I wanted to beef up since my business required me to be physically fit in order to handle the 100-pound sacks of produce. After a few years of intense training I qualified for my black belt, and shortly thereafter a friend and I formed a partnership and opened a martial arts school.

Although my social life, my job, and the karate school consumed most of my time, I couldn't resist a friend's invitation to return to our old high school for a special event being held there one evening. That's where I ran into a girl named Tina Huenefeld, who had been a freshman when I was a senior. I remembered Tina as a shy underclassman who had once dated a friend of mine—but this was not the same Tina. She had literally blossomed during the time since I'd last seen her, and I knew immediately that I wanted to get to know this beautiful young woman. I was thrilled when she said she would go out with me, and

21

it wasn't long before we were steadily dating.

During the time that I dated Tina while she was still in high school, I experienced two significant events in my life. First, my grandfather sold me his small cabin that sat on 12 acres of land just south of Jonesburg. I'm sure Tina's dad wondered why a kid with his own house and business wanted to be involved with his youngest daughter, who was still in school. But I already knew that I loved Tina and wanted to marry her some day.

The second thing happened in the spring, just before Tina graduated, when a gentleman approached me about buying my business. He made an offer that I couldn't turn down, and without giving much consideration to any future plans, I agreed to sell him my business. It's funny how things turn out, but a couple of weeks later a friend of mine who handled my retirement and insurance accounts came to see me.

"What are you going to do now?" he asked.

"I have no idea," I said with all honesty.

"Listen, G.L., why don't you think about coming to work for us?"

I'd never seen myself as a suit and tie kind of a guy, but they were willing to train me, so I figured I'd do that until I found a *real* job. Besides, with the money I now had in the bank I was in a perfect position to ask Tina to marry me. I gave her an engagement ring at her high school graduation, and we were married in my family's church in September of 1986.

It was a beautiful traditional wedding, complete with bridesmaids and all the trimmings. But honestly, when you're a 21-year-old groom and an 18-year-old bride, you anticipate the reception nearly as much as the ceremony itself. We had all of our family and friends with us, and we celebrated with a full-blown band and plenty of drink, if you know what I mean. What a way to kick off the start of our life together.

We settled into the little cabin that I'd purchased from my grandfather, and I dove into my new business life as a financial advisor. At first I felt like a fish out of water. Here was, this young punk kid, trying to give advice to clients two and three times my age. I discovered very quickly though, not only was this a *real* job, it was a real career with incredible potential, something at which I could really excel.

Pretty soon the work ethic that my parents had instilled in me started paying off big time. My hard work and dedication was recognized and rewarded by the company, and within three years I was asked to take a management position in Indiana to open up a new state. Tina and I sold our little cabin in the woods, uprooted our lives, left our families in Missouri, and headed for Indiana. I was 24 years old and things seemed like they were finally coming together for me.

During our first year in Indiana, I broke the company's national sales record. I did it again the second year. As two young newlyweds, Tina and I found ourselves traveling to places we had only dreamed of and making more money than either of us had ever imagined.

From the outside it must have seemed like we had life by the tail. But, on the inside, something was missing. We had been thrust into a world that neither one of us was ready for. We were being treated like adults and we were expected to act like adults. But in reality, we were still a couple of small-town kids living in a big city environment, with no family support system, struggling emotionally as we just tried to function. Tina had a day job, while my job required me to call on clients in the evenings. Not an ideal situation for any young married couple.

We had seen first hand the break-ups and divorces of some of our friends who believed that the grass was greener on the other side of the fence. For them, leaving one spouse and finding another only added to an already stressful situation. A new spouse always comes with his or her own baggage, and sometimes kids from a previous marriage. Unfortunately, by the time couples realize this, the damage has been done already and it's too late to turn back.

Tina and I didn't want to drift in that direction. Our marriage was worth fighting for and we didn't want to throw our hands up in surrender. We decided that finding a church was the answer. Once we experienced the initial relief of being in church again, we fell into an on-again, off-again pattern of attendance. We still enjoyed hanging out with people and doing the Saturday night party thing, which oftentimes left us just too tired to get up on Sunday morning.

As time passed, the initial feeling of isolation we both struggled with subsided as we settled into our new life in Indiana. For the first time we were working more as a team, building a life together, making new friends, and setting joint goals for our lives.

When we first got married, Tina and I knew we weren't ready for kids. Of course, is anyone ever ready? We were married ten years before we decided to try for a child. At first, we weren't too concerned when Tina didn't become pregnant right away, but when four more years passed without a baby, we thought maybe we should look for professional help.

After trying a couple of different fertility drugs without success, Tina was finally prescribed a drug that often results in multiple births. Knowing that twins were prevalent in her family, the doctor cautioned that a single birth was unlikely. I believe his exact words were, "This drug not only works, it works *really* well."

What do you know? Bam! The first month she's pregnant.

We were both so excited. However, Tina's excitement only lasted a couple of days before she became withdrawn and quiet. When I asked her why she wasn't excited anymore, she sobbed, "I'm afraid it's going to be five or six." It seemed an eternity for her until she was far enough along to have her first ultrasound. She was so happy to learn that she was carrying only twins, and not a litter.

It sounds weird to be relieved when you find it's *only* twins. Neither of us had a clue about the amount of work that was ahead of us, not to mention the sleepless nights. I still joke to this day that Tina had been praying to have a child and I was, too. God heard both our prayers and gave us a pair at one time. The moral of that story is, be careful what you pray for, you might just get it.

Although our family of two was about to double in size, my love affair with motocross hadn't diminished. I like to say that it was just on the back burner while the excitement of family matters took center stage. Tina had never openly objected to my daredevil activities, but I could always see the concern in her eyes each time she told me to be careful before I left the house for a ride. Of course, I never was. Besides, I'd weathered the storm of a broken back, which meant I'd already survived the worst thing that could happen to me. A few stitches now and then were nothing to a fearless adrenaline freak.

One afternoon Tina accompanied me to the home of a friend of mine, who owned an excavating company and had plenty of earth moving equipment. Some other riding buddies and I had convinced him to construct a dirt track, complete with jumps, on the back five acres of his property. That track was a real bike magnet, drawing us speed junkies to it as often as we could get away. Common sense said it was only a matter of time before someone got hurt, but common sense wasn't invited that day.

Nobody wants to come up short on a jump. I had already learned first-hand how devastating that can be when I broke my back in 1983. So as I rounded the track for the first time that afternoon, I took inventory of what gear I needed to have the bike in as well as how much throttle would be necessary to clear all the jumps. By lap two, I was in full attack mode and confident that I'd carefully taken everything into consideration...*wrong!*

I sped toward one of the jumps with a vengeance, but I knew the moment I went airborne that I was flying way too fast. Traveling at this rate of speed would put me too long for the landing, which is nearly as dangerous as coming up short. In mid air the front wheel began rising higher and higher until the bike became totally vertical.

I had no choice but to abort a recovery effort. When the bike and I came down, my left leg took the brunt of the impact, snapping my shinbones in half and causing them to protrude through my skin. Needless to say, that smarted a bit. But in my adrenaline-addicted world, a broken bone wasn't *really* broken unless you could see it poking out of your skin—fractures are for wimps.

Thankfully, Tina was on the other end of the property and didn't witness the accident, but she was there when my buddies drove a pick-up onto the track and loaded me for the ride to the small local emergency clinic. When the doctor had to cut off my brand new motocross boot, which hurt me almost as much as the break itself, Tina suggested that maybe it was time to re-think the whole riding thing and learn to take it easy. But neither a splintered leg nor the fact that I was about to become a father affected me.

I was immediately transferred to Methodist Hospital, the largest hospital in Indianapolis. I'd had broken bones before, which only required the standard cast, plus time, equals healing. But this was different; I had a compound break requiring immediate emergency surgery that night. The hospital pinned and bolted me back together, and within four days I was back at home. You know you've done it right when you have so much hardware in your leg that you don't even need a cast.

Even though Tina was pregnant with the twins, she was a good nurse. As I lay on the couch with my leg throbbing, she would eagerly bring me anything I asked for. But by the second or third day of me taking advantage of her good will, she uttered these famous words that I still tease her about to this day: "Why don't you get up and get it yourself? It'll make you stronger."

I hate to admit when she's right, but getting up and around did indeed make me stronger. It still doesn't stop me from giving her a hard time and the long-lasting title of Ms. Compassion. By the time the twins were due, my leg had made a full recovery with the exception of the scars and internal hardware.

All I could think about now was being a new dad. Fourteen years of being without children and living a fairly irresponsible life was about to change drastically. Early on, Tina had made up her mind that she would deliver our twins without pain meds. I believe she was actually afraid of the spinal epidural, but I figured when push came to shove, she'd at least give in to some sort of medical relief. When the time came, she stuck to her guns about no pain meds and delivered our beautiful little girl, Bailey Marie, by natural childbirth.

After witnessing the miracle of Bailey's birth, I learned that one thing is for sure: Tina's a whole lot tougher than I am. But when the doctor couldn't deliver our stubborn boy, Bryce Michael, he had to perform an emergency C-section. Tina is the only woman I know who has been pregnant only once in her life, but has experienced both natural and a Caesarian birth at the same time. Her exact words were, "All that pain for nothing. If I knew I was going to need a C-section anyway, I'd have had them both that way."

Our little family settled into life in Indiana and we joined the First Christian Church of Morgantown. We were still not regular attendees mind you, but we were occasionally present and accounted for, attending only slightly more often than the Christmas-Easter crowd. We were trying to reach out to God, albeit weakly. With the twins, we wanted a greater involvement in the church, bringing up the kids in a Christian environment and a Christian home. We knew this was our window of opportunity to set the example for our children that would last them a lifetime.

Before the kids arrived, Tina and I had purchased a small house in

Morgan County. But as the Bailey and Bryce grew over the next few years, we quickly found ourselves running out of space. We purchased five acres nearby, and decided to build our dream home. This would be the fifth house we had owned since we were married, but the first one we referred to as our "forever home." We moved into the new home in September of 2003, when the twins were almost 3 years old, and for the first week all they wanted was to go home, back to the old house. Moving was no doubt confusing to a pair of toddlers.

Life was good: I had a beautiful wife, two healthy kids, a new home, a great job, and the occasional weekend trek with buddies to ride our dirt bikes through the hills of Indiana, Kentucky, or West Virginia. I had taken full charge of my life and had the freedom to live it to the fullest.

Or so I thought.

NEW BUSINESS — Mid-Missouri Martial Arts Academy has opened a new business in Progress Parkway plaza on the South Service Road in Warrenton. The academy is owned by Jim Hunter, at left, and Gary Woods.

3
From Freedom to Fear

I lived most of my life knowing there were parts of it that were not pleasing to God. I had not only done many things that I wasn't proud of; I'd also done a few things that I was downright ashamed of.

I remember sitting in jail one night, charged with a DWI after being picked up leaving a bar where I'd just watched the NBA finals with some buddies. How utterly embarrassed and stupid I felt. Here I was, a young guy from a great family, spending the night with the kind of people who rob houses or sell drugs for a living. I made a promise to God that if He'd just get me out of the situation, I'd change my ways. He got me out and, as I'd promised, I *did* change. For a while, that is. At that stage in my life, my addiction to adrenaline and the lure of the party scene were much stronger than my desire to live for God.

Even after I was married and became a father, the world had so twisted my reality that I believed I had plenty of time to really change. Deep down I knew that although I attended church on Sundays, I was still living the way the world wanted me to live the other six days of the week. The bottom line was, I knew that I needed to make some major changes in my life, but I wanted to make them on *my* terms and when *I* was ready. I told myself, "I'll make sure to do that before I die," as if I knew when that day would come. I was the one who was in charge of my life and I just wasn't willing to totally relinquish that control to God.

I had no idea when I woke up early on the morning of October 15, 2004, that I was about to find out who was really in charge of my life. For weeks my friend James Fisher and I had been looking forward to heading to West Virginia for an October weekend ride through the rugged coal mining trails of the Hatfield McCoy Mountains. It was a ride we had done numerous times before, and we were excited at the prospect of riding the challenging and technical terrain again. As we drove down from Indiana the night before, we had discussed hitting the trails early to insure a *full* day of riding.

I was ready to go and couldn't wait to get cranking on the first day of our three-day motocross ride. I hadn't slept very well, which wasn't unusual, because I never did the night before a big ride. James had been riding only three years and, typical of some of the other guys I rode with, he didn't want to ride quite as fast as I did. So I knew the day would consist of me riding fast, and then stopping to wait until he caught up. I didn't mind that system at all because when I rode all out, my body welcomed a lot of break time. Even though the terrain was rocky and extremely narrow, these particular mountain trails were the ultimate test of a motocross rider's skills. This wasn't going to be a leisurely ride through a smooth pasture. These trails required an experienced rider with skill and ability. I was keyed up knowing what a great weekend this was going to be.

We were both up early to prep our dirt bikes for the big day. I would ride a Honda CRF 450 and James was on an XR400. We fueled up and did all the final adjustments that were routine for the demanding day ahead.

I never asked God for His protection when I rode, but considering my aggressive riding style, I should have. It was no accident that the number plate on my motorcycle read "911." I was proud to display it, and I jokingly warned my buddies, "Don't try to keep up unless you're prepared to call 911."

Every time I left the house to ride, Tina's last words were always, "Be careful." Even though I would routinely fire back with "I always am," I knew it was a lie. I had no intention of being careful because riding carefully meant *boring* riding. In fact, I had a saying that I often told my friends: "If you're not crashing every now and then, you're not riding fast enough." As insane as this sounds, it's exactly what I thought. When you live by this philosophy, you're gonna go down from time to time. Although that mindset had already cost me plenty of scars and broken bones over the years, it still didn't change the way I thought.

We made it onto the trails early that morning, but then, just 30 minutes into our ride, my gearshift lever cracked. I was stuck in one gear, and I had to nurse my bike back down the mountain to do repairs. James and I both laughed when I told him, "This is when things usually go from bad to worse." We joked that maybe we ought to junk the day and head for the bar. We had already lost four hours of riding time getting the bike trail-ready again, which was frustrating, to say the least. But after lunch the bike was repaired and we were ready to hit the trails again.

The weather that day wasn't very good. The sky was overcast and it was drizzling, which made the rough terrain slick and even more difficult. That didn't bother James and I, though. If necessary, we would've ridden in a monsoon. We both had the fever to ride and nothing could have stopped us.

The particular trail system we had chosen stretched through several counties and was comprised of many steep hill climbs and blind hairpin corners. In almost 30 years of motocross riding, this was by far the most challenging trail I had encountered; it tested my riding skills to the max. West Virginia coal-mining country was known for its rugged terrain, with sections of the trail system so steep and rocky that it was like trying to climb a hillside full of bowling balls. Most places were so narrow as to be impassable on anything that was wider than a 4-wheeler ATV. On previous rides I'd told James, "I hope I never meet another rider coming around one of these turns," not knowing that those words would come back to haunt me.

We headed back up the mountain for the second time that day. We were an hour into the ride, with James hot on my fast and furious trail, when I rounded one of those blind corners. What I saw on the trail in front of me launched a wave of terror—something I'd never experienced before—up my spine as I watched four people on ATVs coming right at me.

In my mind I screamed "Oh no! Stop! Stop! Brake! Turn!" As a result of the frantic move I made to avoid the vehicles in my path, my bike whipped on the rain slick trail, sending me airborne headfirst over the handlebars.

An eerie silence enveloped me as I flew helplessly through the air like a human projectile. Everything seemed to be happening in slow motion, and I could clearly see a rock the size of a beach ball protruding from the trail directly in front of me, about 25 feet away. As I flew nearer and nearer, my mind continued screaming "No!" I realized what was about to happen, and I squeezed my eyes shut a split second before my helmet made contact with the rock.

To this day I can still hear the sound of that bone-crushing impact. Even though the hit was direct and solid to the top of my head, it didn't knock me out. Knowing now what was about to happen, I wish it would have.

As I lay spread-eagle on my back, I looked first to the left and then to the right at each of my arms, and then I looked down at my legs.

I might as well have been staring at someone else's limbs, because I couldn't feel or move them at all. The thought that raced through my mind was, *am I dead?* My mind was working as it always had. Only now it seemed to be attached to a corpse.

Life as I had known it was over in a mere instant. I was hysterical on the inside, a prisoner in my own body, unable to move. I was fully aware of what I had just done to myself, and as I stared up into the murky grey clouds overhead, I can only remember saying with a quivering voice, "Oh no! Oh no! Oh please, Father—no!"

I don't know why I even expected God to recognize my calling out to Him. Up to that point in my life, I hadn't done much to build an actual relationship with Him. But a man knows deep down when he is beyond earthly help. I knew without a shadow of a doubt that I had a major problem here. There is an experience that many people describe as "the moment of truth," which means a critical or decisive time on which much depends. For me, this was my moment of truth.

After spending a lifetime overemphasizing the material things of this world, the things that I'd made myself believe were actually important, suddenly they became absolutely meaningless. I'm sure it's not surprising to anyone reading this book, but at that very moment I didn't have one single thought about how big my house was, what was parked in the driveway, or the amount of money I had in the bank. I would have given up every single material thing that I owned to get my body back.

As I lay on that cold, wet ground with the fall drizzle coming down on me, I can remember having only one recurring thought. *If I can't move my arms and legs anymore, how will I ever be able to hug my family again?* There is no way to describe the horror, hopelessness, and finality of that thought. The weight of it was absolutely soul crushing.

James had been riding too far behind me to witness the crash, but within seconds he came upon the scene. He had seen me crash and burn before, but I'd always jumped right back up and laughed it off. Even though he didn't actually see this one happen, his expression darkened when he recognized the terror on my face, which was also now showing on his face. My voice was shaky and anxious as I struggled to push out the words, "James, I broke my neck. I broke my neck."

While one of the ATV riders went for help, James and another rider each took one of my hands and began to pray. It was unnerving watching them hold my hands, which I couldn't feel, but it was also comforting to know that maybe God would listen to their call for His help. I hoped their communication line with God was better than mine. I kept yelling at James over and over, "I'm scared, I'm really scared." Without trying to console me he said, "Man, I'm scared too, buddy!" My legs were lying over the front end of my bike in such an unnatural position that someone said, "I think you've broken your legs, too."

It was nearly two hours before the rescue crew reached the site of the accident, where they found me exactly as I'd landed, with my helmet still on my head. By then I was extremely cold and my breathing was shallow. The paramedics scurried to immobilize me, putting a hard plastic neck brace on me. The pain from my neck up was excruciating, making the process of loading me onto a backboard nearly unbearable.

James screamed at one of the paramedics, "Hey man! Watch what you're doing!" This particular guy was a *big* man that James described as being a couple of Twinkies shy of 300 pounds. When I later asked James why he'd snapped at him, he said, "When I looked down, the guy was standing in the middle of your hand." I didn't fault the paramedic. There wasn't enough room on that trail for everyone at the scene, and besides, I couldn't feel anything.

With my helmet still on my head, the paramedics secured me

onto a backboard and loaded me onto a 4WD utility vehicle for the arduous trip to the bottom. I've never experienced such pain. Had I been able to feel the same intense pain that was in my neck with my whole body, I probably would have blacked out.

The trip down the mountain took about an hour, but it seemed like a lifetime. The sensation I experienced with every bump, twist, and turn of the uneven rocky trail was like a thousand knives being stuck in my neck. The rescue team gave me the standard "you're going to be all right" talk all the way down. I understood they probably didn't want to say what they were really thinking for fear it would panic me even more. But they weren't kidding anybody, I knew this was as bad as it gets.

Coming down off that mountain was just the beginning of my journey. The poor weather conditions had created an extremely low cloud ceiling and limited visibility, which grounded all Med-Evac helicopters that day. It was an unfortunate perfect storm of events that prevented me from getting timely medical attention, which is crucial for a spinal cord injury.

Since the helicopters were unable to fly that day, an ambulance was waiting at the bottom of the mountain to take me to Logan Hospital, a small emergency facility about an hour's ride away on a curvy, narrow, bumpy road intended for use by coal trucks. I was so scared and nervous during that ambulance ride, yet I held on to a thread of hope that there would be something the doctors could do. Surely they'd be able to operate or do *something* for me. After all, hospitals are in the business of fixing people—and I'd always been fixed before.

During the seemingly endless trip, I tried to imagine what it would be like to function without the use of my arms and legs. How would permanent paralysis impact Tina and our kids? I thought of how I'd always bragged that I had no fear of anything. That wasn't entirely true. There was one thing I feared the most, and that thing had just happened to me.

Having never truly experienced fear before, its presence was both unfamiliar and unnerving. Just a few hours earlier my entire life had been played out like a newsreel running through my mind. But now, fear had just changed the reel. I recalled tormenting images of people who were confined to wheelchairs, some so immobilized that a straw-like device, made for sucking and blowing, was required just to drive their chair. Visions of quadriplegics with tracheotomy tubes in their necks haunted me. I couldn't help but ask myself, "Will that be me the rest of my life? Is that what I'm going to look like?"

Ironically, the actor Christopher Reeve had passed away only five days earlier. The star of the Superman film series had become paralyzed in 1995 as the result of a horseback riding accident. During the onslaught of the news coverage that week, numerous video clips of him were shown; images of a frail and rigid man strapped into his wheelchair. His neck tilted backwards into his chair's head support, and every breath seemed to be a struggle as he wheezed through his ventilator. I vividly remember thinking to myself, *What a horrible experience that must have been for him, to have lived the last ten years of his life like that.* So, naturally, I had felt a sense of relief that his nightmare was now over. I couldn't imagine living my life in that condition. Now, less than a week later, that's exactly where I was: paralyzed—just like Christopher Reeve. *His* nightmare had come to an end, but mine was just beginning.

Upon my arrival at Logan my helmet was finally removed, I was examined, and a few tests were run. Although I was happy to learn that my legs were not broken, they were the least of my problems. The doctors were unable to determine whether I'd actually broken my neck or, worse yet, if I'd severed my spinal cord. Clearly, my injuries were beyond their expertise. The fear that I'd managed to keep at bay for the past few hours began once again to rise up within me, and the newfound sense of isolation I felt in a strange hospital, so far from home and everyone that I loved, only added to my despair. I felt as if I'd just fallen into a bottomless pit and was, unmercifully, sinking ever so slowly into fear's dark lair.

James had stayed at the crash site to help with the efforts to get our motorcycles and equipment down the mountain and loaded onto his truck before returning to the lodge to gather our personal belongings and check out. Needless to say, I was relieved to see his familiar face when he finally arrived at the hospital. His presence helped to ease the sinking sensation I'd been experiencing.

"You've got to call your wife and let her know what's happened to you," James said. Tina and our twins had gone to Missouri to visit family for the weekend while I was riding. She was not expecting to hear from me until the ride was over, and even though James insisted that she needed to know, I told him that I didn't want to call her yet. James must have asked the doctors and staff to lean on me because they, too, started pressuring me to inform my wife. All I could say to them was, "I'm just not ready."

At least I had control of something.

Thankfully, neither James nor any of the hospital staff knew how to get in touch with Tina, who was with my brother, John, and his wife, Julie, or I'm sure they would have done so. Although the total extent of my injuries was still unclear, I knew that life as Tina and I had known it was over. I was trying to wrap my head around the conversation I would have with my wife. What would it sound like? What would she say when I told her what I'd done?

The beautiful and vibrant memory of everything that we'd done and everything that we'd built had just shriveled to irrelevance as I faced a new vision of our life. All I could see at that moment was Tina pushing my head—the only part of me that was alive—around in a wheelchair for the rest of my days. At the same time an eerie voice inside of me repeated over and over again, "Gone. Gone. *Gone!*"

After just a few short hours, they told me I was being transferred to a larger hospital in Huntington, West Virginia. I took this as good news, knowing that I would now have access to the kind of specialized technology and medical expertise that I needed. The downside of the transfer would be the more than two-hour ride in another ambulance, which was unavoidable since the medical helicopters were still grounded due to the weather.

When I arrived at the Huntington hospital in the early morning hours, nearly twelve hours after the initial crash, I was still strapped onto the wooden backboard that had been put beneath me on the mountain trail. Because of the severity of my injury, the emergency personnel had been afraid to remove it. I longed for the comfort of my wife's touch. I tried to imagine what it would be like to have her caress my now *dead* hands. But right then, the only thing that would resemble comfort was a total stranger running a warm washcloth across my face.

With each hour that had passed since the initial impact, I'd become increasingly more anxious and agitated. I could read fear and deep concern on the faces of those trying to take care of me, which only fueled the sense of hopelessness and despair.

"Mr. Woods, I want you to wiggle your toes for me," the ER doctor said.

I put everything I had into the effort, and was pleasantly surprised when I actually felt my toes move. "How's that?" I asked. The grim shake of the doctor's head told me that there had been no movement.

"But I felt them move," I told the doctor. He explained that what I felt was called a phantom movement, nothing more than my mind playing tricks on me.

I sunk deeper into despair as I realized that I couldn't even control my toes, much less my life.

The emergency room personnel immediately ran CT scans and MRIs of my neck in order to assess the extent of my injury. At last I would know at what level my spinal cord was damaged and if the cord was severed.

It wasn't long before the intensive care doctor came in with the test results. His expression was as grave as I've ever seen on a person's face. I tried playing dumb as I asked him, "So how long am I going to be paralyzed?" I really just wanted to cut to the chase and find out where things stood.

"I'm so sorry, Mr. Woods," he said, "but there's nothing we can do for you. You've sustained a major contusion to your spinal cord at the critical C3 level, and there is no reversing it."

I couldn't believe what I was hearing; I had actually done the unthinkable. The doctor's words were surreal, like a line straight out of a TV doctor show. He went on to say that they still couldn't tell if I'd broken my neck or severed my spinal cord. I wasn't afraid of a broken neck, because I knew bones could be fixed. What I didn't realize was that a spinal cord doesn't have to be severed for a person to become paralyzed. Most paraplegics and quadriplegics haven't actually severed their spinal cords, but the result is still the same.

Now, after years of all-out-no-fear riding, I had just become one of those wheelchair people who had once tugged at my heartstrings. People were going to be looking at me with sympathy in their eyes, and I didn't know if I could face that. I'd never thought that I would ever crash so badly that I wouldn't recover from it.

I just wanted to be left alone and not have to deal with anyone. Knowing how desperate I was, the doctor said, "I can only imagine how you must feel, and I'm sorry we can't do more for you. But you need to consider yourself a very lucky man. Considering the severity of your injuries, we don't understand why you didn't sustain a hangman's break of your neck."

I was puzzled, "What does that mean?" I asked.

"Let me tell you like this: hangman's breaks don't usually make it to the hospital."

What! How can you die riding motocross? I thought to myself. *Is that possible?* I was just going for a weekend ride, something I had done hundreds of times. My mind struggled to comprehend the magnitude of what I was hearing.

I was lucky to be alive, I guess, if you could call this living.

I was in the Huntington ER about six hours before I was moved into an intensive care room where they finally moved me off of the backboard that I'd been on for the past 18 hours. I was totally exhausted, yet during the previous 24 hours I'd found it impossible to sleep.

I had nothing but time to think about and relive the horror of that mountain. The crash was continually replayed in my mind as I pictured different scenarios.

What could I have done differently?

Should I have gone left, or maybe right?

Should I have braked harder—no, softer?

I was driving myself insane with all the "what ifs." It really didn't matter what answers I came up with; they changed nothing.

I was into day two of my paralysis and I still hadn't called my Tina. How was I going to break the news to her? How would I begin? What would I say? I was 39 years old, and we'd been married for over 18 years. We had just built our dream home a year earlier, and the twins were getting ready to turn four. I couldn't bring myself to tell her that I'd just destroyed our family. She had no clue about what had happened the day before. As far as she knew at that moment, James and I were a couple of days into our ride while she and the kids were busy visiting family in Missouri. Making the call was by far the toughest thing I would ever have to do.

I nervously awaited James' arrival that morning. When he entered my room and opened his mouth to speak, I immediately cut him off. Although I was on the verge of backing out on my decision to call Tina, I blurted out, "It's time!"

James didn't bother asking what I meant; he already knew. The initial look of relief on his face quickly changed to urgency as he grabbed the phone. He fervently dialed the number I gave him and held the phone to my ear. With each ring of the phone I became more fearful and unsettled. If I had been able to physically hang up the phone, I would have. When Tina finally answered and realized it was me, she was so happy and excited to hear my voice. Fear tightened its grip on me, and her tone quickly changed when she sensed distress in my voice.

"What's wrong?" she asked.

"I'm in the hospital."

For a few seconds she may have thought I was kidding.

"Are you okay?" she asked.

My voice got shaky as my emotions began to surface. "No, not this time," I said. Even though I'd rehearsed what I was going to say, I ended up blurting out "I'm paralyzed from the neck down."

The phone got deadly silent. Tina started to cry and then I heard her say, "What? No!"

I found myself using the same line on her that the paramedics had used on me, "It's going to be all right," even though I knew what I was saying wasn't true. Things were by no means going to be all right. I did my best to comfort her, even though I knew it wasn't working.

"I'm on my way," she said. "I'll be there as quick as I can," she kept repeating.

As we hung up, we both said, "I love you." Not the bland I love you that married couples sometimes utter routinely; this expression was deep and heartfelt, from the soul. Tina was on her way to me in West Virginia, and for one brief moment I felt the comfort of knowing that my wonderful wife would soon be at my side.

But that ray of hope grew dim as fear once again moved in like a thief, stripping my soul of any semblance of peace, and surrounding me with a shroud of darkness so heavy that I struggled to breathe. I was utterly alone, without hope.

Maybe it would have been better if I'd just gone ahead and died on that mountain.

4
When Time Runs Out

Over the years I've tried to describe how I felt when I learned that my situation was permanent. To say I was devastated would be the understatement of the year. While I found some moments of comfort whenever one of the doctors or hospital staff was in the room with me, the time I spent alone was living hell.

Fear was my ever-present reality, and with it came a mental torment so vile that I felt as if I were constantly sick to my stomach—although the doctor would likely have told me it was just another phantom sensation. Well, this phantom was with me 24-hours a day and the only way I could envision myself getting free from its powerful grip would be through the mercy of death.

I never had any thoughts of suicide, but I recalled a man who had lived in a nearby town when I was growing up. He'd had some sort of accident that had left him a quadriplegic, and I remember that he got around in a power wheelchair. One day he drove his wheelchair into the path of an oncoming train and ended his life. At the time I remember feeling sorry for him, but now I wondered if he had experienced the same kind of torment and hopelessness that I was feeling.

Time had just run out for the once fearless G.L. Woods. I knew that this time I wasn't going to be able to fix myself, and neither was the medical community. My despair was further fueled by my belief that God had just thrown me in the trash. As I considered my life up until that point, I can honestly say that I'd given Him every reason to do just that.

After growing up with a good Christian foundation, I had drifted away from my Lord. I was living with worldly motives and intentions. Oh, I would still make it to church from time to time, depending on how rowdy Saturday night had been. But, church attendance was more off-again than on-again. I was very much playing the game of church, thinking I could show up once in a while, you know, make my appearance, which qualified me to be a Christian. Showing up at church for my tour of duty an hour each week no more made me a Christian than standing in my garage made me a mechanic. Instead of striving to build a genuine relationship with my Lord and Savior, I was just going through the motions. I took up space on the church pew with my body, but sadly, I never took up much space with my heart. I had been deeply deceiving myself.

For all the blessings I had been given, I'd never once expressed my gratitude to God. I had convinced myself over the years that I was a nice guy and a hard worker. Therefore, I felt deserving of all the good things that had happened; I had earned them. It's funny, though, you never read in the Bible that nice guys get to go to heaven. Nice has nothing to do with turning your life over to your Creator.

I was deep into my one-man pity party, asking over and over again this question: why me? Then I would think, *why not me?* I was neither better than anyone else, nor was I immune to tragedy anymore than the next person. Truth be told, I already knew the answer to the question, why me? In the past, the only time I'd called on God was when I needed something; like when I got into trouble with the law, or when my marriage was faltering, or when my grandfather was dying. I just wanted God to hear my plea and then fix things so I could continue my life without the emotional pain, as if He were some sort of a cosmic bellhop.

Even though I didn't think God bargained, it still didn't stop me from trying to play Let's Make a Deal. This time the only difference in the game was what I pleaded for: "Father, if this is the life you now have in mind for me, then I beg you—*please* let me die!"

Needless to say, it turned out to be yet another unanswered plea.

After I talked to Tina, James began contacting friends and his own family in Indiana, telling them what had happened. Eight of our closest friends immediately dropped everything and headed for West Virginia. With Tina and the twins in Missouri, with my brother John and his family, our friends were closer and would arrive before Tina. However, my parents were celebrating my mom's birthday in southern Indiana that weekend, and it turned out that they were actually the closest to me. Tina urged them to immediately head to Huntington. She knew they could get there quicker than everyone else, and after hearing the desperation in my voice she understood just how badly I needed my family. The waiting had begun. I couldn't rush Tina's journey, but I needed her there badly.

Tina and John loaded their bags and immediately left on the ten-hour, 525-mile trek to the hospital, which meant they wouldn't arrive until late that night. Since my brother would eventually have to return to Missouri, they traveled in separate vehicles while the twins remained in Missouri with John's wife, Julie.

With no company in the car to console her, I can only imagine what must have gone through her mind during that seemingly never ending car ride. The helpless feeling of not having any control over our family's future must have been excruciating for her. I know it was for me. I learned later that at one point, at least 300 miles from Missouri, Tina had stopped to refuel the car. When she went in to pay, she was told that someone else had already paid for the gas. John wasn't with her at this stop and Tina was among strangers. Why, at this moment of her need, would someone do this? She had not talked with anyone about why she was traveling. No one knew her story, her need, or the situation. But maybe, just maybe, God did.

I had already spent endless hours lying motionless, with the exception of my head, alone and isolated for the most part because visitation was limited in the intensive care unit. It would still be hours before anyone arrived, so I spent my time mulling over every single word I'd overheard from the medical staff as I'd listened for any glimmer of hope. But most of all, as I stared at that ICU ceiling, I contemplated my life's mistakes and shortcomings, as well as the bleak future ahead of me now. I still couldn't imagine living life as a quadriplegic, although I tried to visualize what that would look like. I made the decision to mask my true feelings before anyone arrived. It would have done no good for everyone to be as scared as I was.

In addition to having gone without sleep for more than a day, I was also medicated and somewhat groggy. But I recall the sense of relief I felt when my parents arrived. I could tell from the look on my dad's face that he was near tears, which hurt me deeply. I had only seen him cry one other time in my life, and now I was the reason for *both* times. I knew that Dad had a good friend from the army who became a quadriplegic, and he must have known what a tough life it was for his friend and what it might mean for me moving forward. No one wants to imagine what that would be for a loved one.

My mother tried to stay positive. Some mothers would have fallen apart or been hysterical, but that was not her way. Mom was tough.

After all, she had been in the army, which is where she met my father when they were stationed in Germany.

It's funny what comes to mind during times of great stress. I remembered the time when I was a kid that Mom showed me the trophy she'd won for getting first place in the army's sharp-shooting competition. I'd never seen Mom pick up a gun, but that day I thought both she and the trophy were the coolest things ever. That is, until she told me that on the day of the competition there was a big snowstorm in Germany, and she was the only competitor that showed up.

Mom had purposed to stay strong for my sake, trying to keep me focused on recovery. Somehow, she felt in her heart that everything would be okay. I kept thinking she was nuts. Throughout life, when certain things happen, you know deep down that they will work out and be fine. But this was different; things weren't just bad, for me they were utterly hopeless.

Our group of friends arrived a few hours later, and although it gave me great comfort to know that they cared enough to come and be with me, all I really wanted was to see my Tina. Then, ten hours after we'd said good-bye on the phone, Tina walked through the door and was finally by my side.

Because of the fatigue I was dealing with and the pain medication they were giving me on a continual basis, the details of that evening are a blur to me. But one thing I do remember is the look of distress on Tina's face. My heart ached because of the pain I had caused her and my family.

Even though I couldn't feel her touch, when Tina sat on the bed and held my hand it brought a new level of comfort that dispelled the fear and darkness—even if only temporarily. Our familiar exchange of "How ya doin' Babe?" had no place in these circumstances. How could we console each other when dealing with such total devastation? There just wasn't anything to say. We would have to face this together, but right then it was too painful and raw to deal with. She gazed at me so sorrowfully as she caressed my hand. I would have given anything at that moment not to witness the sadness that I had caused expressing itself so painfully on her face.

ICU wouldn't allow my family to stay by my side for any length of time, so they were often down the hall in the waiting room. Stress was already at a peak level for friends and family because my blood pressure and heart rate would drop to dangerous levels when I slept, coupled with my shallow breathing. Everyone froze with fear when the ICU unit called a code blue over the intercom, which meant one of the ICU patients' hearts had actually stopped. The room was dead silent while they nervously waited to hear if it was me. Fortunately, when it wasn't, everyone breathed a sigh of relief.

Throughout the night everyone tried to remain upbeat. However, as if the original injury wasn't bad enough, they learned that I now faced a new threat. Pneumonia. The doctors were clear: pneumonia was a battle that I couldn't afford to fight. I was already devastated and distraught. How much more fight was in me? Both my grandfather and Tina's grandfather had died from pneumonia. It was so painful to watch them both struggle for each breath they took, and I didn't want to die that type of death.

With my weakened respiratory function, even the simplest task, like drinking water, was terrifying. I didn't even have the ability to cough because of my paralysis. This meant if I choked, I could literally drown while drinking a glass of water. Since aspiration is the biggest contributor to pneumonia, this was a real threat, especially since I was only receiving liquids. My respirations remained shallow, so when I needed to cough, staff or family would do what was called a buddy cough. This was done by someone performing a chest compression on me as I attempted to exhale.

Nights in the ICU were the worst as I lay alone while the rest of the hospital slept. During those times, I tried to will my fingers and toes to move. I watched carefully, trying to catch any glimmer of a twitch. As strong as my will was, my body still refused to respond. As much as I welcomed the escape from reality that sleep brought, I quickly came to dread the awakening process. My first conscious thought was usually that I'd just experienced an intense and highly detailed nightmare about being paralyzed, and I was relieved that it was over. In reality, the living nightmare began again and again each day with the realization that the frightening events forever embedded in my mind were not a nightmare—they were real.

How was I going to live like this? Where was I going from here? Everything my life had previously been was over.

In a genuine effort to try and lift my spirits, Tina had brought our camcorder with her, thinking it would help me to see videos of the twins. Unfortunately, what I saw was myself playing with them on the floor, chasing them and throwing them into the air, the twins in a chorus of giggles and laughter. This only confirmed what I was already thinking; those were things that I would never experience again.

In the past I didn't always stop what I was doing when the twins wanted Daddy to play, because I was too busy. At that point, I would have given anything to be able to throw them into the air again or wrestle them around on the floor. Why do we all take such simple yet meaningful things for granted?

Hour after hour, nothing was changing, and by Sunday evening my support system was dwindling. My dad and brother had to return to Missouri for work. Our eight friends from Indiana had to go back home to their lives, leaving me to deal with what was now my life. My mom had originally planned to go back with my dad and brother, feeling that she needed to be with our three-year-old twins, who were still in Missouri, clueless as to what had happened to Daddy. She felt we had enough to deal with without having to worry about the kids, too. I was relieved when, at the last minute, she decided to stay with Tina and me.

At some point that day it occurred to me that it was her birthday. Before going to West Virginia for my bike ride, I had sent her a card with a note that said, "I'm sorry we won't be spending your birthday together." Well, here we were—happy birthday Mom. How ironic.

Tina and Mom took turns spending time in my room day and night throughout the next 48 hours. When not on duty with me they slept, or what barely resembled sleep, in the waiting room. By now, the staff at Huntington Cabbell had done a good job of caring for me and keeping me stable, but beyond that, there was nothing more they could do.

I was desperate for hope. Wasn't there *anything* more that could be done? All I knew was that I needed to return to Indiana. Tina and I made the decision to transfer me to Methodist Hospital in Indianapolis. After all, Methodist was a huge facility with the latest technology, and they'd fixed me before. Surely I'd find new hope there.

Indianapolis was too far for transport by helicopter. Going by ambulance would have taken eight hours and could have damaged my spinal cord even more, so the hospital put us in contact with a medical airline. Tina and the hospital staff began coordinating with this company, making plans to transfer me to Methodist. It would be very expensive for the 727 medical jet to fly me back to Indianapolis, and my insurance company was adamant; *they would not cover this huge expense.*

Tina was concerned about how we were going to pay for the flight and all of the expenses that go along with the care needed in transit. But she understood it wasn't a matter of money; it was a matter of need. We would work the financial details out later. The pilot kept reassuring Tina not to worry about the cost; he knew she had a full plate already. His genuine compassion is just what she needed at that moment. We still don't know how it happened, but months after our flight we learned that the insurance company did, in fact, pay the bill in full.

The original flight scheduled for Monday afternoon was repeatedly postponed because the jet was needed for other emergency calls. Monday afternoon turned into Monday at 5 p.m., then 7 p.m., then late Monday night, then Tuesday morning. I was ready to go, anxious for the answers I desperately needed, but I felt that time was working against me. How critical was rapid response to my situation?

My mom had left earlier that afternoon. She drove to Indy and planned to meet up with us at Methodist Hospital ER. I was worried about mom driving the eight hours back to Indy with little to no sleep. She had to be exhausted, because I knew I was.

Again, the weather conditions were not ideal. It was overcast, rainy, and chilly. Some time Tuesday night, after a painful trip to the airport by ambulance, I was quickly loaded onto the plane and we were on our way. A full medical staff was on the plane, but I was their only patient. A little over an hour later we touched down in Indy. I was both scared and hopeful at the same time. Maybe a new hospital, especially one with the reputation of Methodist, would provide me with that miracle that I so desperately hoped for.

We arrived at Methodist around 1 o'clock Wednesday morning. Not that anything had changed in my condition, but it was still comforting knowing that I was back home. I was hoping they could find something that would make me whole again.

I was whisked through the back entrance of the hospital, which was reserved for the most serious trauma patients. The corridor we entered had a creepy feel to it, perhaps because fear was a constant visitor there. The long hallway was painted a pale green, it was dimly lit, and it smelled of chemical antiseptic. I listened to the quick clicking sound of the gurney wheels as they flew over the tile floor heading for the ICU. I was traveling so fast that I could feel a gentle breeze on my face as I was rushed along. This was my third hospital in six days, and as with each transport, I always felt like only my head was being moved from place to place. The rest of my body was dead.

There was no comparison between Methodist ICU and what I had experienced in West Virginia. This facility had a much more intense, critical feeling. Before my arrival, I had started to calm down some, but the feeling of intensity brought back all my anxieties—only now at a higher level. The personnel had such grave looks on their faces that it scared me even more. I asked myself, "Am I still going to die?" Maybe that would be the best thing for me.

I hadn't been allowed to drink anything since the previous afternoon. I was so thirsty. I repeatedly asked for water, but in the event that I might require surgery they wouldn't allow it.

Within the next 48 hours I would know my life's fate. They re-ran all the tests—MRIs, CT scans, and other nerve tests—trying to determine the extent of my injury. Since I was in intensive care, I had a constant barrage of doctors and nurses in and out of my room, so the lights were always on. In a room with no windows, every hour was the same. With nothing to do but wait for the next test, I spent my time concentrating on trying to move my fingers and toes or counting the ceiling tiles, anything to pass the time.

I was allowed to have visitors for only five minutes each hour, leaving me feeling more and more lonely and isolated, with the exception of one unwelcome visitor—*fear*, who had followed me from West Virginia. For 55 minutes out of each and every hour, fear made its evil presence known. I watched the clock constantly, looking forward to my next five-minute visit with Tina or my mother.

Once she was satisfied that I was settled into ICU, my mom left for Missouri to bring the twins home to Indiana. I wanted to see them so badly, but I was also afraid to see the scared looks on their faces when they saw me. The Daddy they knew was always roughhousing with them and throwing them into the air. Now he was immobile and vulnerable, not the way any dad wants his kids to see him.

Tina stayed at Methodist Hospital with me until Wednesday evening before making the one-hour drive back to our home. She told me later what an eerie feeling it was coming into the quiet, empty house without the kids or me. Sometimes you don't realize what a joyful noise a family can make until you walk into an empty, silent house.

My hope in Methodist was short-lived. All of the test results came back with the same conclusions as at Huntington Cabell: I was going to be a quadriplegic. They still weren't sure whether I had actually severed my spinal cord, not that it mattered. Severed or not, the prognosis was the same: "We're sorry, there is nothing we can do for you." It was then that reality set in for me. If Methodist couldn't fix me, then my condition really was permanent. *This is it; I've actually done it.*

On Thursday afternoon I was moved from ICU to a regular room, further enforcing the reality that medical science had run out of options for my recovery. If there was an upside to the move, it was that I could now have unlimited visitors and eat real food.

For the first week following my crash, I wasn't allowed any solid food. The only nourishment I received was through an IV. While I was looking forward to a meal, at the same time I was terrified that I might choke on anything solid that was put in my mouth. My diaphragm was still partially paralyzed, which meant I would be unable to cough if I were to choke.

How ironic that after riding all those years with no fear, now just the mere thought of eating food frightened me.

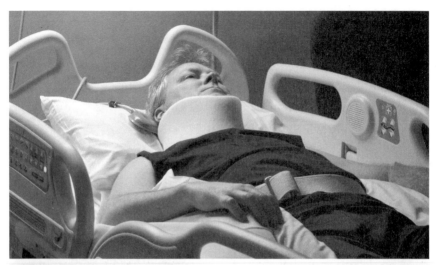

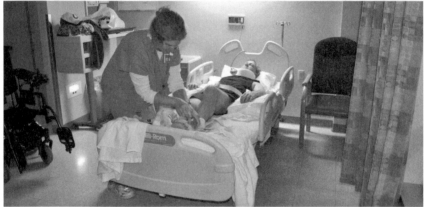

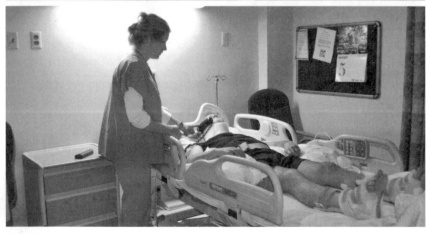

5
Last Chance

The specialists at Methodist explained that going directly to my home following my stay at the hospital was not realistic, which explains why, sadly, some patients are left with no choice but to relocate to a nursing home. I needed to be someplace where I could learn how to live as independently as possible as a quadriplegic, and they recommended the Rehabilitation Hospital of Indiana.

An acute care and rehab hospital, RHI specializes in brain and spinal cord injury, offering comprehensive medical rehabilitation for injuries that result in loss of function. Because of their renowned reputation, nearly 5,000 patients come through RHI's therapy program annually, including injured Indy 500 and NASCAR drivers who often recover at the facility. I was transferred to RHI on Saturday—just eight days after my accident.

Upon my arrival at RHI, I caught a glimpse of the therapy gym as my stretcher passed by the open door. My therapy would begin on Monday, leaving me the weekend to wonder what they could possibly do for someone like me who was totally paralyzed. I'd already accepted the fact that starting Monday therapy would be my new job, my new place of business, every day from 8 a.m. to 5 p.m. for the next several months.

As my stretcher was whisked down the hallway toward the spinal cord wing, I saw the silent stares of patients watching from their wheelchairs. Their facial expressions seemed distant and cold as they checked out the new guy, but I'm sure they were just wondering how my injury occurred and the extent of my paralysis. Or maybe they were just having flashbacks of their own arrival at RHI. In the coming months, I found myself doing the same thing with new patients who were admitted. Welcome to Club Med.

I was placed in a two patient room in the spinal cord injury wing of RHI. It was now eight days since my crash and every stop along the way was hurry up and wait for the inevitable conclusion, "There is nothing we can do for you." Would RHI be any different? There was no therapy on weekends, so I would have to wait until Monday morning to find out.

I wondered how many patients had previously occupied this bed, looked out this same window, and felt the same fear I was experiencing. How many are home now, living a different life? How many successes? How many disappointments? Knowing that the stream of needy patients would never end, I asked myself the bigger question: how many more patients would come after I was gone?

I had never personally known anyone who was paralyzed, and now everyone in my immediate vicinity was paralyzed either from the neck down or the chest down. Not surprising, most injuries were from vehicle accidents, but there were a few freak accidents, such as the lady who had been trying to slim down by riding a stationary bicycle in her living room. She had tripped while getting off, hitting the floor and leaving her paralyzed from the waist down. Or the man who fell off his ladder while doing routine gutter cleaning, leaving him a paraplegic. The most shocking was the lady who had been vacationing in Florida with her family when she became ill. Within hours of her arrival in the ER she became paralyzed from mid-chest down due to spinal meningitis, which had attacked her spinal cord.

All of these situations drove home the point to me of how fragile the human body actually is; it was a revelation that I wouldn't have believed a week earlier. While you could expect someone racing dirt bikes or cars to sustain a serious injury, these folks were just going about everyday life. Regardless of how the injuries were sustained, everyone in that wing was living the same nightmare.

I watched out the window of my room as family members and friends came and went, visiting patients, some with hope, and some with none. A few patients were also outside in their motorized wheelchairs. I especially noticed those who were strapped into their chairs with head supports, their feeble hands barely able to control the joystick that enabled them to navigate the sidewalk. My heart went out to them, but the reality was they were already far beyond what I was capable of doing. I remember thinking, *oh, those poor people,* before I caught myself and realized I *am* one of those people now.

The visitors were also struggling in their own way, trying to find a way to cope with their loved ones' new reality. The resilience of these families was impressive. I'm sure many tears were shed in private, but there was no crying at RHI.

I couldn't help but think of all the things I would never be able to do again. I would never run again, ride a motorcycle, hug my kids, or make love to my wife. I had taken so much of my life for granted, and in an instant it was all taken from me. What kind of life was I going to have now?

I tried to settle into what would be my new routine at RHI, even though everything seemed foreign to me. I was given a large button that was pinned to my pillow, which I was to use when I needed to call for a nurse. To activate the call button I had to roll my head onto it. If the button wasn't in the correct position, it was useless because I couldn't move to reach it. For the first time in my life I was totally helpless, a 39-year-old infant. The old mentality of "if you want it done right, do it yourself" flew out the window on that mountainside. Now my every need depended on someone other than myself. It was a bitter pill to swallow.

Even though there was a phone next to my bed, what use was it to me? All I could do was stare at it. Unless someone was in the room to answer the phone and hold it to my ear, I had to tolerate the incessant ringing until the caller gave up. While being unable to answer was frustrating, I was at least comforted knowing someone cared enough to call.

My mother had returned to Indiana with the twins the day before I was transferred to RHI, and Tina planned to bring them to see me a few days after I arrived at the facility. It would be the first time I'd seen them since the crash, and I could hardly wait for them to arrive.

I thought about them constantly, wondering how they would react to this new dad. It was sad to think of the many times I had wrestled with them, throwing them up in the air with their hair flying and their nervous grins of uncertainty as they landed back in my arms. That old dad was gone forever and I knew it, but 3-year-olds wouldn't be able to comprehend it. I still didn't know what this new dad was going to be. Would I be a piece of furniture in the corner of the room, strapped to a wheelchair so I wouldn't fall out? Running and chasing them around the yard or throwing a football with Bryce wasn't going to be our future together. But what would it be? Only time would tell. I felt Tina and the twins had been cheated. The crash had been a freak accident, but wasn't I to blame for taking the risk with their future in the first place?

All this weighed heavily on my mind on the day that the twins were coming for their first visit with me. Finally, I could hear them coming down the hall, their excited chatter to each other and Tina. As soon as they rounded the corner into my room, the brakes came on and the chatter abruptly stopped. Their little faces went blank. Their eyes were large and staring. They stood rigid and motionless in the doorway, and I believe they would have backed out of the room had it not been for Tina standing behind them encouraging them to keep moving. They had always seen me as strong, virile and taking charge. Now I was different. Dad appeared frail, weak, and he was most certainly unable to move.

The sight of me lying in that hospital bed must have been incomprehensible to them, shocking in its reality. Daddy's face looked the same but the rest of him just wasn't right. I couldn't even open my arms to them for a hug. They kept their distance and wouldn't come near the bed. Their faces registered the fear they felt, while I was trying not to show mine. Tina and I kept encouraging them to come near the bed, but it was just too overwhelming for them. I understood how they felt, but I was so hurt and afraid they wouldn't come near me. It was as if they had never seen me before; Daddy was a total stranger. The man in the bed sounded like Daddy, but everything else was different.

Over the course of several visits, they eventually accepted the situation and, like all children, resiliently adapted to their new Daddy. I could always hear them coming from a long way down the hall, like an approaching freight train. I would hear Tina calling to them to slow down and stop running. Only now they would jump onto my bed and Tina or Mom would wrap my arms around them so they could feel Daddy giving them a hug back. I couldn't even feel them lying beside me, but my heart definitely experienced the touch of those little snuggly bodies.

Now, I'm an adult and cartoons aren't really my thing, but to have those kids snuggle up with me in bed to watch Bugs Bunny was heaven. That was mental therapy time for Daddy. I lived to hear those little munchkins racing down the hall with Tina corralling them into my room. That was what I needed to fight for, as normal a life as I could provide for Tina and the kids.

※※※※※※※※※※※※※※※※※※※

It was make it or break it time for me. I would either gain some mobility or live the rest of my life as a quadriplegic. My future depended on what happened now. On Monday morning I began what was to become my regular 6:30 a.m. wake-up routine. I was catheterized, fed, my teeth were brushed (which was pretty weird), and my hair was combed. Try to envision a total stranger responsible for the most personal needs of your life, like a kindergartner going to school for the first time.

Getting me dressed was a major ordeal. Imagine trying to clothe an uncooperative life-size wet noodle as the nurses tugged, pulled, lifted, and turned me in an attempt to make me presentable. Not that it mattered much, I wasn't going to a fashion show—I was going to work. They put my shoes on, which I thought was bizarre since I couldn't walk. Why bother? I never knew why, but I believe it was a simple way of helping me return to a familiar routine.

For the first time I was about to experience life in a wheelchair. Like most people, I could never have comprehended a wheelchair being a major part of my existence. But now it was reality, a very surreal experience. I was 5'11" and 200 pounds, and two small nurses were going to transfer me, a wobbly mass of Jell-o, from my bed into that chair. It would be a major undertaking.

They reached around my waist and fastened a gate belt, a wide heavy canvas strap that the staff could grip as they moved me from

64

place to place. I felt like I was a human suitcase and it scared me. What if they dropped me, lost their balance, or the chair moved on them? I certainly couldn't catch myself in a fall and would end up a heap on the floor. Or worse yet, I could break a bone. I couldn't afford any setbacks at this point. Trust them or not, I was totally in their hands, and to my surprise they quickly got me into the wheelchair. Once I was strapped in, so I wouldn't fall out, I was wheeled down the hall toward the gym.

It was 8:00 a.m. and I was entering my new world as my wheelchair and I went into the large open rehab gymnasium for the first time. I was both scared and excited. I knew that any progress I made here would impact the rest of my life.

Reality wasn't pretty as I looked around at the other patients with various levels of injury and recovery. The gymnasium had slept over the weekend, but it exploded Monday morning. I was surprised at all the activity and people, both staff and patients. There were nearly 60 patients dealing with brain injuries, strokes, and, like me, spinal cord injuries. Some were inpatient, others outpatient, coming back for additional therapy. But they all had the same goal: trying to regain normalcy in their lives. Even though I knew I had a real problem, I remember thinking as I looked around, *thank God I wasn't a brain injury patient*. I at least knew who I was; I was just trapped in my body.

I looked around the room for patients like me, who were suffering paralysis. I watched and wondered at the various aspects of their therapy. No one knew to what degree I would be able to function. Everyone was poised to help me, but no one knew if the game could be won or how many innings it would take.

My physical therapist was a petite and bubbly woman named Leslie. She had an upbeat personality and I quickly found out that she was surprisingly strong. I wasn't just a job to Leslie; I felt that she was really on my side, wanting to help me all she could. Her compassion for my situation was real and heartfelt. She explained that her role in my recovery would be to focus on my torso and leg movement, although at the time there wasn't anything for her to work with. She stressed the need for setting goals and asked what I wanted to accomplish while at RHI.

"I want to walk" was the first thing I blurted out, "that's my goal."

"Whoa, whoa, whoa, time out," she gasped. "Let's not get carried away. How about we start with baby steps, setting more short-term goals?"

To appease her I then set three goals, which were being able to scratch my nose, use a TV remote control, and hit the call button for the nurses' station. We finally agreed that to begin, the goal of therapy was *moving something*—even if only twitching a finger or wiggling toes. Movement of any kind was the basis to build on. It was hard to imagine how only a finger twitch could turn into something positive and, in my case, life altering. But I had to begin somewhere and I was ready to start.

Monday was evaluation day, designed to see what I was able to do that they could build on. I would like to have been a mind reader when they learned that I had nothing to offer them. It was impressive to me that they had a game plan, even though I couldn't get on the field yet. Try to imagine developing a starting point for someone with zero movement. My brain would tell my arm to move, but I might as well have been talking to someone else's arm because nothing happened. Like a rebellious teenager, my own body wasn't listening. I kept wondering how all of this therapy was going to help—what could they possibly do for me?

Following my evaluation, Leslie then grabbed my gate-belt and with a solid heave-ho she transferred me from my wheelchair onto a large elevated 8' x 8' foam mat. That mat and I would get to know each other really well over the coming months. Leslie began by manipulating my joints, rotating and moving my legs, ankles, arms and elbows. It was hugely important that I maintain flexibility to avoid muscle contractions, which I was powerless to prevent on my own. The scourge of paralysis is muscle tension that causes the wrists, fingers, ankles, and feet to draw up. As I scanned the gym I could see that this had already afflicted other therapy patients, and I knew I wanted to avoid those pitfalls at all cost.

My occupational therapist was a woman named Amy, a caring, professional person with a warm, humorous personality. Our personalities blended well together and we hit it off from the get-go. She was ready to build on the slightest movement of my hands and arms, if and when that day ever arrived.

Amy didn't allow any pity party. It was time to get to work and, with Amy, work was fun. I was wheeled up to a chest high table where Amy's tools of the trade resided. There was a hand pedal bicycle, blocks, and other toys that a baby might play with such as Silly Putty, boxes that were divided in the middle, skateboards for your arms, stretchy therapy bands, and other things whose usefulness I couldn't even imagine. Over the coming months, I would become *very* familiar with all of them to the point I would be sick of looking at them.

I would sometimes see a patient ring a bell hanging on the wall and the whole therapy gym would stop and erupt in cheers. I learned that as patients reached small therapy goals, they would ring the bell to let everyone know progress was being made and to encourage those still struggling. I wondered if I would ever reach any goal and get the chance to ring that bell.

Because of the paralysis I didn't know when my bladder was full and I had no sensation of needing to urinate. I'd been catheterized since the day of the crash, but now at RHI they didn't want the catheter to remain permanently inserted because of the possibility of infection. Despite my paralysis, up to eight times a day I would have to endure the discomfort of having the catheter inserted and removed. The staff was insistent that I drink a lot of water throughout the day to keep the kidneys and bladder flushed. I fought this knowing that shortly I would have to be catheterized again. Not just for the discomfort, but for the modesty issue as well. It didn't take long for me to understand I would have to check my dignity at the front door.

Getting true rest was almost impossible because my body needed to be rotated every two hours, day and night, to relieve pressure points and prevent bedsores, which are the plague of a quadriplegic. Nurses would come in to perform the exhausting schedule of roll center, sleep, roll left, sleep, back to center, sleep, and then roll right. For the next few months there was no such thing as a full night's rest. A healthy person doesn't realize how crucial this sleep movement is to the human body. We naturally move and rotate our bodies without even being conscious of it. Ironically, Christopher Reeve had survived the trauma of his spinal cord injury for ten years, but died as the result of not being able to recover from the blood infection caused by his bedsores.

In addition to being constantly moved while in bed, I also had to wear boot braces to prevent foot drop, a common affliction of quadriplegics that causes their calf muscles to draw up and pointing the toes down. Left untreated, foot drop can become irreversible, making it impossible even to place the feet on a wheelchair footrest. My hands were similarly treated with forearm braces from my elbows to my fingertips to keep them straight and prevent them from curling under.

Trying to sleep with these apparatuses was annoying, and I wondered if they were truly necessary. I was still wearing the neck brace that the paramedics had put on me when I was brought off that West Virginia mountain. A nurse would prepare me for sleep fitted with the hard plastic neck brace, tight fitting orthopedic stockings, hard plastic boots, hard plastic arm and hand braces. If I were lying on my side, my back was supported with pillows and another between my knees. No wonder I only got two hours sleep. As if that wasn't enough, the nurse had the nerve to cheerfully wave on her way out the door, saying, "Get some rest now," as I grumbled to myself —*whatever!*

A man and his TV remote is a heavenly marriage, but even this was denied me. Changing channels on the TV was almost impossible. A device attached to my bed rail held a tube that arched over towards my face. By either blowing into the tube or sucking on it, the channel would go up or down. Using this device was much harder than it sounds. It took practice for me to be proficient, but it was actually kind of cool. This was my first experience with technology that allowed me to do something for myself.

Mealtime at RHI reminded me of the twins as babies, when I would spoon food into their mouths. The big difference was, now I was the infant, wearing a bib and needing someone to put food into my mouth. It was a time-consuming process that couldn't be rushed because swallowing was still difficult and scary. Food and water still made me uneasy because of the fear of choking. Unable to cough on my own, I still would occasionally need staff assistance with a buddy cough. As I would weakly try to cough, the nurse would sharply compress my chest, quickly forcing air out of my lungs. This sounds like a really crude method, but it was effective. I hoped as time went on my diaphragm would wake up enough that choking wouldn't be an issue.

In the evening, those who were able to sit upright were gathered around a table adjacent to the nurse's station for dinner. The paraplegics could at least feed themselves; the rest of us had to be feed. Having to be fed was humbling, to the point of embarrassment. But looking around I knew I wasn't the only one. We all looked like babies with food and drink spilled down the front of us.

I wanted so badly to be able to do things for myself. But it was always a waiting game; waiting for someone to have the time to feed me or perform any other simple task I needed to have done, like scratching my nose or turning a page of a magazine. The staff did the best they could, but I was just one of many patients, and we were all in need.

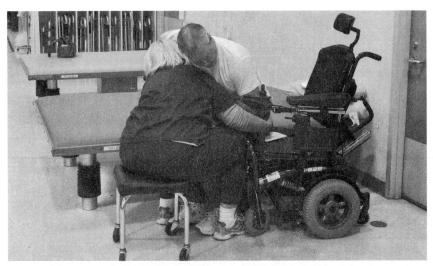

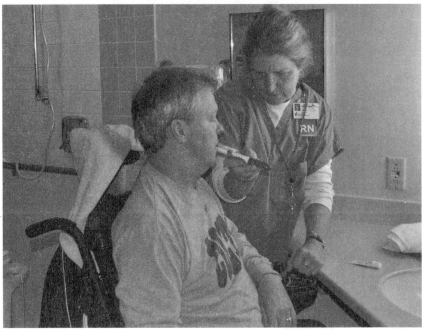

6
God Works in Mysterious Ways

Tina had an incredible ability to maintain a normalcy of life for Bryce and Bailey, who turned four years old just two weeks after my accident. We decided that we'd have their birthday party at RHI so I could share their special day with them.

We reserved an empty conference room for family, friends, and kids that we'd invited to join the celebration. Tina did a beautiful job of transforming the clinical hospital atmosphere into a comfortable party room for four-year-olds. Balloons, cake, and presents abounded. I tried so hard that day to tune out everything else that I was dealing with and just concentrate on their party. I wanted to enjoy *their* day, but as I sat strapped into my wheelchair, I couldn't help but wonder if this was how all of their future parties would be.

Four-year-olds in a birthday party setting didn't realize that the adults were only putting on a party face that day. After all, we were there at RHI because of my tragedy and all that it meant for our family's future. Everyone tried to put away their heavy hearts for the two giggling twins, even if it was only for an afternoon. I don't believe the children felt one bit cheated as they enjoyed their cake, their birthday cards, and lots of presents.

The twins were not the only ones who received cards that day; I also received several encouraging cards. Friends and church members started sending cards and notes on a regular basis, and before long mail was arriving from other parts of the state and eventually other parts of the country. I began receiving cards from people I didn't even know, total strangers. At one point I even received a card from someone in Japan. How had they heard of me? Why would they take the time to do that? How could these people have so much compassion for me, someone they had never met? I was touched and strengthened by their outpouring of love and support.

As the old saying goes, "God works in mysterious ways." A friend of mine who lived in Minnesota attended a church pastored by Jeff Utecht, the father of Indianapolis Colts' rookie Tight End Ben Utecht. When Jeff mentioned he was going to Indianapolis to watch Ben play on Monday Night Football, my friend told him about me and suggested that if he had time, he should stop by to see me at RHI. I was totally taken back when, on Sunday afternoon, both Jeff and Ben Utecht showed up in my room. Ben was all decked out in Colts blue and I was thrilled. He brought a signed Colts hat for me and both he and his dad expressed their sincere concern about my condition. Before leaving they both held my hands and prayed for me.

Ben gave me his cell phone number and told me that if I ever wanted to come see a Colts game, to call him and he would hook me up with tickets. By the time I would be in any condition to physically be able to take him up on his offer, another football season would have already passed. Right now I couldn't even move my toe, much less think about going to a professional football game. Still, his offer gave me hope.

Sometimes, if the weather was decent, a friend or family member would take me outside in my wheelchair. The first time I visited the garden area of RHI, I noticed a row of bricks with people's names engraved in them lining the sidewalk. At first I thought these must be the names of RHI patients who had passed away, until I realized the bricks also said "Patient of the Year" followed by a date. I learned from a staff member that these were people who had shown exemplary fortitude and perseverance toward their recovery process. She told me the name of the sidewalk was The Pathway to Independence, but some simply referred to it as God's Sidewalk.

God, do you really walk and talk with people today, like you did with the first man and woman in the Garden of Eden?

In the weeks to come, I started picking out patients in the therapy gym who I thought would be good candidates for the Patient of the Year award. From the beginning, it was obvious who the fighters were and it was just as obvious who had been beaten down by their circumstances.

In addition to the names memorialized on the Pathway to Independence, in the hallway outside the therapy gym was the Wall of Fame. That is where former patients shared their stories about their time at RHI and what successes they were able to achieve. There were numerous stories told by Indy 500 and NASCAR drivers who had rehabbed at RHI after various crash-and-burn accidents. Sports figures, celebrities, and just normal people like me had told their stories as an encouragement to current patients, giving hope that a productive life beyond RHI was possible. I scoured every story looking for those that were similar to my own, desperately seeking inspiration for my own journey.

At that point in time, the finality of my paralysis hadn't completely sunk in. I still couldn't envision living the rest of my life as a quadriplegic. I remember telling myself, "I can't live like this." As I looked around at other patients, I actually found myself envying those who were paralyzed *only* from the waist down. At least they had the use of their arms, which meant they could feed themselves, navigate in a wheelchair, and, most importantly, they could hug their families.

I had nothing.

Everyone has heard the saying "You don't have to look very far to see someone worse off than you." This is a fact that unexpectedly slapped me in the face one day when a young man about my age, whose name was Jesse, was brought in on a stretcher to share my room.

Jesse's girlfriend had shot him in the neck during an argument, leaving him completely paralyzed. The incident had happened more than twenty years ago, and Jesse now lived with his mother who cared for him. She appeared to be around 70 years old, and was a sweet, caring woman. It couldn't have been easy for her sharing his living nightmare.

Jesse was tall and thin, with arms and legs that shockingly resembled pencils. His atrophy was so severe that his hands had curled permanently into tight fists and his feet pointed unnaturally straight out from knee to toe, like a ballerina on point. It was then that I truly understood the importance of wearing my foot and hand braces at night. It dawned on me that this is what they'd been trying to prevent from happening to me. All of my complaining about having to wear the devices stopped abruptly that very day.

Jesse had a newly implanted medicine pump that would help reduce his muscle spasms. When his doctor came to see him later that day, I overheard him say that Jesse would be there for a few weeks, and while at RHI they would like to get him sitting up in a wheelchair. Then the doctor bluntly asked Jesse, "When was the last time you sat up?"

Jesse replied, "1997."

I was stunned. That meant he'd been lying flat on his back, 24 hours a day, for the past seven years. When I heard that, I wanted to cry. While I had been living my life, playing with the twins, working, and driving a car, Jesse had been lying in a bed unable to move. What had he been doing for the past seven years? I knew how much I hated staring at the ceiling after only a few weeks—but doing so for seven years was unimaginable.

I tried several times to engage Jesse in conversation, but he was literally a man of few words. If I asked him a question, I'd get a one-word answer, never much more. Understandably, Jesse was at times sharp with his mother and the RHI staff, who were only trying to be helpful. But who was I to judge? I hadn't walked in Jesse's shoes for the past 20 years.

Although I saw Jesse a few times in the therapy gym, I got the impression that he felt therapy was useless. By the time he left RHI a few weeks later, the staff had him sitting in a reclining wheelchair. But even this small improvement in his daily life was of no interest to him. The fact was, Jesse had given up. I decided right then and there that I would neither allow myself to become embittered by my situation, nor would I ever give up hope of walking again.

What right did I have feeling sorry for myself? If I had to live the rest of my life in a wheelchair, I would still have it easier than Jesse. I didn't know if Jesse had his own relationship with God or not—and I wasn't sure if God would even listen to me—but I felt a need to pray. "God, please comfort this man" was my heart-felt prayer as I forgot about my own circumstances and needs and focused, instead, on the needs of someone else.

God had just opened my eyes.

Even though I had been struggling for years with my own Christian walk, it was at that moment that God spoke to my heart, assuring me that I would be okay. I knew that being okay didn't necessarily mean I would walk again. But, I told myself, "However this is going to turn out is just going to be the way it is." And for the first time, I was okay with that. I was finally at peace with my situation, and I had genuine trust in God's plan for my life. I wasn't able to read or turn the pages in the Bible that was in my room, but I recalled a scripture verse that I'd heard only months earlier in church. *"For I know the plans I have for you," declares the LORD, "plans to prosper you and not to harm you, plans to give you hope and a future"* (Jeremiah 29:11).

In the past I'd heard people say that God spoke to them, but I never fully understood what they meant. "What! God spoke to you? I'm sorry, but I'm not hearing anything." It was there, at RHI, where it became clear to me that God speaks to our hearts, not our ears. Once I understood that, I realized He had been speaking to me for a long time. Either I wasn't listening or I had the volume turned down. I'd always been far too busy doing my own thing, too absorbed in *me* to hear Him.

It was then that I knew I wanted to make it, and I was going to do whatever it took to not only just live, but to *thrive*. I would commit myself to my therapy and work as if my life depended on it, which it did. I would never quit or worry about how long my rehabilitation might take; I was on fire. God had used Jesse to do this for me.

Although I knew that God could do anything, I didn't want Him to just snap His fingers and have me jump up and walk. That would be too easy. Most of my life had been pretty easy already, and all it did was cause me to become arrogant, taking every blessing I'd been given for granted. God was going to allow me to work for my miracle, and I was okay with that. I was ready to fight.

Just as the staff at RHI needed me to give them something that they could work with, some small movement on which they could build, so it was with God. He needed me to give Him something that He could work with, and that something He needed was my faith.

Even though Philippians 4:13 says I can do *all things* through

Christ who strengthens me, I was hearing the verse in a stronger way—I can do anything, *anything* through Christ who strengthens me! This became my anthem, and it ran through my head literally hundreds of times each day.

❦❦❦❦❦❦❦❦❦❦❦❦❦❦❦❦❦❦❦❦❦❦❦❦❦❦

When I was at RHI, it meant the most to me to talk to someone who had walked in my shoes, someone who had been through what I was living. The doctors, nurses, and therapists could only relate what they had learned from textbooks; I wanted first-hand recovery experiences. So, I was thrilled when the staff first approached me and asked if I would like to meet with a young man who had sustained an injury similar to my own.

Justin was a guy a little younger than me, who was married and had a stepson a little older than our twins. He had spent two months at RHI and had been released from the facility only a month before I arrived, but he was still returning to RHI for outpatient therapy.

I was told before I met him that Justin had been paralyzed following a diving accident. Unaware that repairs were being done at a familiar diving spot, he dove into a lake, slamming his head on a large steel pipe that had been placed a few feet below the surface of the water.

When I saw Justin walk through my hospital room door I was elated. Finally, here was someone who had been paralyzed, too, but unlike me he was walking. Okay, so he wasn't walking perfectly, but with the help of a walker, he was at least on his feet. The first thing that caught my eye was the metal halo that was bolted to his head to provide support for his neck. It looked cumbersome and uncomfortable, but despite that he still seemed energetic, upbeat, and genuinely enthusiastic about life. This was exciting, my first real sense of hope for a normal life.

Justin knew exactly what I was going through as he asked about the heaviness and the pins and needles sensation up and down my arms and legs. We discussed the desperation of wanting to move—to move anything. We spoke of time frames of his progress. I wanted to be able to gauge myself by his successes.

My first visit with Justin was exciting because it gave me something that I could add to my newfound faith: it gave me hope. The Bible say that *faith is the substance of things hoped for, the evidence of things not seen* (Hebrews 11:1 NKJ). Although there wasn't yet any evidence in the natural that I would ever be able to move again, I fully believed that I would walk out of RHI when my time there was complete.

Over my remaining time at RHI, these visits with Justin were pivotal to my recovery. I could see, with my own eyes, what might be possible for me. He may have tired of me cornering him in the therapy gym with my endless barrage of questions, but Justin was always gracious and I was always encouraged by our conversations.

Over the following weeks I slowly started coming back emotionally. The overwhelming presence of fear and torment that had suffocated me since the accident had left the moment I'd heard God say that I was going to be okay. In its place was a welcomed sense of wholeness, which was not surprising considering what the Bible says: *For God has not given us a spirit of fear, but of power and of love and of a sound mind* (2 Timothy 1:7 NKJ).

With the bleakness and darkness no longer a part of my life, my old silliness and sense of humor began resurfacing. Therapy wasn't just a job now, but a place to also have fun and cut up. For the first time since the crash I was finally able to laugh at myself again, while my body comically struggled to do what my mind was telling it to do.

Part of my therapy with Amy consisted of her attaching electrodes to my forearms to stimulate the muscles to movement. When the current pulsed, my hand would involuntarily flex upward at the wrist. That's why I named this piece of equipment the Frankenstein

Machine. I growled like Boris Karloff while my claw-like hand rose and fell on its own.

I told Amy, "This is a waste of crucial therapy time unless I'm planning on playing the part of Thing on the Adams Family TV show."

Amy laughed and said, "Trust me, Grasshopper!"

There is an old cliché that says you have to crawl before you can walk, but at that time even crawling seemed out of reach.

Each day after visiting hours were over we had a lot of down time, and I remember lying in bed trying to make my fingers move. I would focus and strain on that, all the while declaring my favorite scripture that I had personalized just for myself: I can do *anything* through Christ who strengthens me. I wanted so badly for my fingers to just twitch, even a little bit.

One evening during this nightly ritual, the index finger on my left hand moved, ever so slightly, but it moved. I was stunned. Something had actually moved. *Did that really just happen? Oh my God, it moved, it moved!*

I tried again, and it moved again. This was no phantom movement; I'd seen it with my own eyes. That one movement, as slight as it had been, was monumental for my mindset. I spent the rest of the evening twitching that finger up and down. I couldn't wait for the next morning so I could demonstrate for the doctor what he said would never happen: I'd show him *the finger*.

My newfound faith and the joy I'd felt as a result of my first victory was quickly challenged by two incidents that occurred in the same week. The first came when I was I was visited by a social worker who was adamant about signing me up for Social Security disability. Her reasoning was that because it was a time-consuming process to get my application approved, the sooner we started the sooner I would be receiving benefits. I was just as adamant that I was *not* going to apply for disability because I was going back to work. She all but rolled her eyes at me. I'm sure she had seen situations like mine before, and had therefore already presumed the outcome. That's why her paperwork was all but complete when she came to see me; all she needed was my signature on the dotted line. I could see that she had absolutely no faith in the possibility of my recovering.

The second challenge to my faith occurred when four guys representing the local wheelchair rugby team came to talk to me. I'd heard the therapist talk about this team, and I could tell they were enthused and excited about their visit. They referred to their sport as "murderball" because the players usually became rough to the point of people flying out of their wheelchairs. They told me about the league, the tournaments, and the matches, and they said as soon as I got out of RHI, I could bring my wheelchair and join them. It would be a lot of fun.

As they continued to bubble over, I just kept thinking, *whoa, wait a minute. I'm walking out of here.* Without being blunt, I tried to convey to them that I hoped I wouldn't be in need of a wheelchair when I left RHI. They quietly stared at me, unable to respond, probably remembering their own initial hopes for recovery. I totally understood they meant well, but their visit just reinforced my determination to work even harder.

I don't know who suggested that this team visit me. I'm sure whoever gave the okay had the very best intentions in mind, but I was blindsided by their visit. I wasn't prepared for what they had to say, and quite honestly the visit scared the crap out of me. I felt like I was being forced to look down the road of my life and see myself forever in a wheelchair.

I spent a lot of my down time that week contemplating everything that my doom-and-gloom, doubt-and-despair visitors had said to me, wondering if I was deceiving myself into believing that I would leave RHI on my own two feet. Then one night, as I was channel surfing with the help of my custom remote device, I came across a program that featured a popular televangelist. It was as if the words of Jesus that he was reading from the book of Mark were intended just for me. *So Jesus answered and said to them, "Have faith in God. For assuredly, I say to you, whoever says to this mountain, 'Be removed and cast into the sea,' and does not doubt in his heart, but believes that those things he says will be done, he will have whatever he says"* (Mark 11:22).

As I closed my eyes to go to sleep that night, I whispered, "I can do *anything* through Christ who strengthens me—including walking out of RHI on my own two feet."

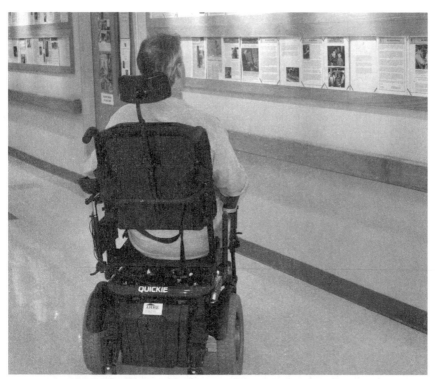

7
Turning Point

I started telling the therapists and staff that when it was time for me to leave RHI, I planned to walk out the front door. It undoubtedly sounded ridiculous to some, and a few nurses gave me what I considered to be "the look," a sad gaze that spoke volumes. They didn't have to say anything; you could read it all over their faces. It was the look that said, "Please don't do this to yourself; don't set yourself up for disappointment. " I dismissed the look with a mental *whatever*. I was on a mission.

Each person involved with patient care at RHI was truly awesome. Everyone needs to make a living doing something, and we patients were their job. But their interest in our recovery went so much beyond that. They shared with genuine empathy our stresses, struggles, heartaches, successes, and failures. They were our teammates, cheerleaders, and coaches, doing their best to get us back into the game of life, whatever position we may have to play.

All of us patients had reached the bottom of our emotional barrel, the darkest hours of our lives. The staff had to deal with that in their own way. Day after day, week after week, year after year, the stream of patients was unending. They just kept coming. Even at the end of each day as the staff left us and went home to their families, somewhere out there, people were becoming their future patients. Like grass that grows as you sleep, car crashes would never stop, riders would continue to be ejected from ATVs and motorcycles (or as my mother calls them, murder-cycles), and unexpected freak accidents would happen. It's a 24/7, 365-day-a-year business. Life-altering trauma never takes a day off. In that branch of the health care field, human nature would say that you must disconnect from that world to be able to survive any length of time. The staff not only didn't distance themselves emotionally from their patients, they plunged in with their whole heart and we felt their genuine compassion.

After only a month at RHI, I'd already regained minimal muscle control of my arms. It wasn't much, but my hope was that I could progress to actually feeding myself again. Toward this goal, the staff hooked me into a feeding apparatus. This feeding assist was on a rolling stand that arched over my head toward the dinner table. Hanging from the top of the stand were huge rubber bands that were attached to each of my wrists. As my arms dangled from the bands, the therapist strapped a spoon and fork into each hand. The utensils had foam sleeves the size of an empty toilet paper roll; this would help my hands to grasp. This unit was intended to combat my ever-present enemy, gravity.

I was a marionette moving in slow motion, a puppet on a sophisticated string. Both the apparatus and I were out of control as I wildly swung to and fro trying to hit my mouth with food. As Mom used to say, "That's a good way to put an eye out." I had tried to tell them I wasn't ready for this, and from the looks of the food on my shirt, my lap, the table, and the floor, I was right. But, this was the first baby step to my independence and I was willing to endure it. No, it didn't work real well at first, but eventually I was able to get more food in me than on me. Progress was being made, but initially it wasn't pretty.

Shower time at RHI was an event like no other. The bathroom was huge in order to accommodate wheelchairs. Strapped butt-naked into my wheelchair, I was regularly rolled into the tiled room and hosed down in what I'm sure looked like a scene from a prison movie. I almost expected them to powder me with a scoop of lye disinfectant, like in the movie *Shawshank Redemption*. Sometimes either my mother or Tina was recruited to be the shower Nazi for this humiliating duty. Whenever I would get a new roommate, I'd always be sure to keep a straight face as I soberly informed them, "You're gonna love shower night." When that shower door closed on them for the very first time, I would be lying in bed giggling.

Without a doubt, the whole hospital and rehab experience was the most humbling time in my life. Never before had I needed to count on so many people for my very existence. It brought to mind Luke 18:14, which says, *for everyone who exalts himself will be humbled, and he who humbles himself will be exalted.* Up to that time, I had spent the biggest part of my life exalting myself, patting myself on the back. What could be more humbling than to have a total stranger feed me my food, brush my teeth, or wipe my rear end? Hopefully, not at the same time. Yuk!

Unlike the hospitals, RHI allowed unlimited visitors, and they started showing up immediately; not just my family members, but friends and church family as well. Not one day went by that someone other than family was there to visit. RHI provided my physical rehabilitation, but family and friends were my mental rehab.

The shock of seeing me for the first time registered on the face of a number of my friends. I could see they didn't know what to say. Some friends would have to carry the conversation when others were too stunned and literally speechless, as they tried to comprehend my situation. I never understood how crucial true friendship was until I needed it as badly as I did then.

I remember the day that three out-of-state friends, Jude Hopper, Joe Miller, and Dave Hellman, blew into my room as excited as three rowdy high school sophomores. It was just what I needed: comic relief with a capital C. They hadn't seen me since the crash and no doubt were shocked, but they never showed it. They had brought me lunch from Burger King, complete with the paper crown, which they put on my head. They dumped me into my wheelchair with two pinwheels attached to the back of it, slapped a pair of sunglasses on me, and we raced down the hallway heading to therapy. I had been crowned king for a day, and was seated on my mobile throne with pinwheels spinning and my buddies giggling like schoolgirls. I looked like a dork and I loved it.

In therapy that morning, Amy put my arm on an apparatus that resembled a small skateboard. My orders were to sweep my arm back and forth across the table. I broke out in a sweat from the sheer effort of trying to move my arm even a few inches. As I struggled, Jude stepped up to my therapy table, taunting me with "Come on girly, show us what ya got!" With everything I had, I swung my arm across the table and caught Jude square in the groin. He doubled over in pain as I laughed unsympathetically. "You got what you deserved," I said. "Look who's girly now!"

That same morning, Amy was in the process of transferring me from my wheelchair onto the elevated therapy mat, positioning my wheelchair near the mat and placing a board bridge under my rear end. While she tugged on my hands, I did my best to scoot my body onto that bridge to the mat. This was a long and grueling process, resulting with me only moving an inch with each effort. But I made it.

Amy had just gotten me seated on the mat, and for the first time I was actually sitting on my own. She became so excited that she turned away from me to yell out to those around us. "He's sitting! G.L. is sitting on his own!" she exclaimed as all eyes were on us. Everyone else was excited, but the only thing I felt was my body slowly beginning to collapse backward onto the mat. With no ability to support myself, my head and body bounced as I hit the mat hard like a ton of bricks. The only thing bigger than my eyes were Amy's as she swung back around toward me and realized what had just happened. I was seeing stars and I was mad at her. "What the heck were you thinking, Amy?"

My buddies' initial reaction was, like mine, shock. But when they realized that I wasn't really hurt, they did what all good friends do; they laughed their tails off. On the other hand, Amy was embarrassed and apologetic all day. My response was, "No harm, no foul." To this day, Amy and I still laugh about that incident.

Having my friends beside me in therapy that day was uplifting. But the reality was that when we went outside to the courtyard to have our Burger King lunch, the men that I'd hung out with for years had to physically feed me. This was the new reality we had to share, which had to be especially sobering for my friend Joe Miller, whose brother, Louie, had recently passed away. More than thirty years earlier, Louie had just graduated from high school with a full football scholarship. On graduation night he was in a car accident that had left him paralyzed from the neck down. Joe had experienced firsthand the life of a quadriplegic. He knew better than anyone the kind of life I was facing.

Before his visit, Jude Hopper had taken the time to dig out a bunch of old pictures of the four of us that had been taken over the years. They were a timeline of all the goofy things we had done, a real trip down Memory Lane. Because our families had spent so much time together, the photos were a reminder of just how close we were. Only really close friends allowed you the comfort to act like a complete idiot without embarrassment.

There must have been 50 pictures on a large poster board of our families together and individually. Each picture brought back a special memory, and even some pain, as I realized that these experiences may never happen again, certainly not in the same carefree manner we had once lived them.

The poster board hung on a wall next to my bed throughout my stay at RHI, and I only had to turn my head to relive what had been. I would spend hours looking at those pictures, picking them out one by one, replaying in my mind how each day had unfolded. The photo was only a snippet of the whole day and the memories it had entailed, such as riding Harleys in Hawaii, scuba diving in Puerto Rico, and countless days of boating and skiing at the lake. There may have even been a photo or two of the guys *mooning* the camera, but you didn't hear that from me.

Through this picture board the staff was also able to see me in a life other than my present one, in which I was lying frailly in bed unable to move. They had only known me one way, and that was being wheeled through the front door on a stretcher. Now they were able to see that I'd had a life before RHI, and it was healthy and vibrant.

The board always attracted people, visitors and staff alike. It was a focal point in my room that got lots of chuckles and laughs. "Nice butts" was the number one comment people would make when they noticed the moon shots. Even the novice student nurses were sent to the board to check out the "assets."

Another highlight for me was my weekly visit with my friend James Fisher, who was with me on that mountain in West Virginia. He would always offer to bring me something from the outside world. RHI food was good, but you can't beat a good juicy steak dinner. James, who not so long ago was racing with me through the mountains, now had to feed me like an infant. It was weird. Not just James, but other friends showing up at meal times as well, would be recruited to feed me. We had always been rough and tough guys, used to hanging out doing guy stuff. It was unnerving to feel so vulnerable, frail, and helpless as they spooned food into my mouth. It hadn't been so long ago we had been living life on the edge.

Life sure does take strange turns.

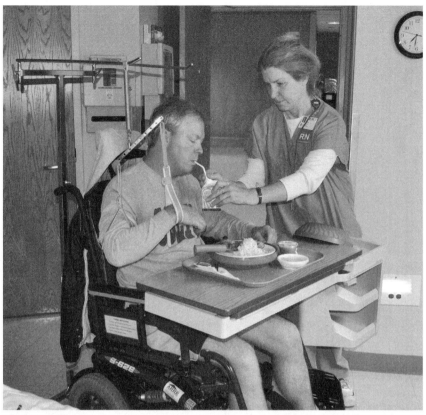

8
A Mission of Faith

I had become accustomed to the pattern of first-time visits from those who wanted to show their support. At the sight of me either lying in bed or strapped to a wheelchair, smiles always gave way to a flood of conflicting emotions. Shock, fear, dismay, and denial were just a few of the emotions that registered on the faces of friends and family alike, who were undoubtedly thinking, "How can this be happening to someone I actually know?"

The day my friend James's dad, John Fisher, walked into my hospital room, I was expecting nothing more than another first time visitor. I was prepared for the initial look of surprise followed by the usual visitor conversation. "How ya doing?" "How are things going?" "How's the food here?" Run of the mill typical stuff. Knowing John as I did, I should have known better.

John had always been a direct, forthright, no-nonsense, type of guy. You always knew where you stood with him because he'd tell you straight to your face. Some people were uncomfortable with this type of personality, no pussyfooting around for John, because he was honest to the point of bordering on rudeness.

93

I firmly believe that John *knew* why he was coming to visit me. I think he came with a plan about what our conversation would include—something a whole lot deeper and profound than just small talk. Because of what James had shared with his dad about the dark days we experienced together immediately following the crash, John understood the gravity of my situation better than most people.

Past the small talk, I shared with him the thoughts and feelings I'd experienced as I lay on that mountain, and about the ER doctor who came to me in the Huntington Hospital. John listened patiently as I relived the horror of that day.

"Lying in the ER I was already totally distraught when that doctor told me my injury was irreversible. I almost wished I had died on that mountainside," I said. "And then the doctor went on to tell me, 'Mr. Woods, I'm sorry we can't do more for you, but you need to consider yourself a very lucky man. Our team of doctors has looked over your scans and charts and we can't for the life of us figure out why you didn't sustain a hangman's break of the neck.' When he explained that hangman's breaks don't usually make it to the hospital, I was shocked. John, I wasn't supposed to die that day. I was just going for a weekend ride, like I'd done for years, and…"

It was then that John stopped me in mid-sentence and said, "Let me ask you something, G.L. If your life *had* actually ended that day, would you have at least been ready?"

I was stunned by his candor, which caught me totally off-guard. Was I ready? It took me a few seconds for the question to register in my brain. Truth be told, I didn't know. I wasn't sure. I averted my eyes and answered, "I…I don't know."

I could see that John was somewhat perturbed by my answer. Being the Christian man that he was, I could tell it wasn't what he wanted to hear.

"Let me tell you something, *boy*" John boomed. "If the answer to that question is I don't know, then the real answer is no!"

I felt like someone had dropped a ton of bricks on me. What did he mean? After all these years of church going, surely I was prepared to meet my Maker, wasn't I? I most certainly believed in Him. Besides, hadn't God spoken to me and told me that everything was going to be okay? Hadn't I been making miraculous progress in my rehabilitation? Hadn't God been showing me how much He loves me?

The Bible says *If you declare with your mouth, "Jesus is Lord," and believe in your heart that God raised him from the dead, you will be saved. For it is with your heart that you believe and are justified, and it is with your mouth that you profess your faith and are saved* (Romans 10:9-10 NIV). In an instant I knew the truth: *Oh my God, I'm not ready!*

I understood the cost of not being ready had I died on that mountain. That mountain cost me my body, but my failure to be *ready* could have cost me my soul. Mark 8:36 puts it this way: *For what good is it for someone to gain the whole world, yet forfeit their soul?* What had I really been living for? I realized that for all these years I had been taking up space in the church pew with my body but not my heart.

I knew that I was at a crossroads of life at that moment. I sent up a silent, desperate call to God: *Oh Lord, please help me!* I guess you could say it was my "Faith 911" call. And God answered that call immediately through John Fisher. Our conversation immediately turned to what did I believe about God and what I should do to be *ready*. I don't think John ever realized what an impact our conversation had on my life from that point forward. That day was truly life changing for me. *Thank you, John, for coming to me when I needed you the most and I didn't even know it. Your courage and faith were touching.*

As Christians, we don't always go through doors that have just been opened for fear of offending someone. But John strode purposefully through that open door, on a mission of faith. Even though we should never underestimate how what we might say or do could impact another person's life, we still sometimes take the easy or safe route and say nothing. John was to have none of that. He wasn't afraid to tell me what I really needed to hear.

I explained to John about being baptized in my hometown church when I was 12 years old. I was a kid, so it didn't feel like it was a life-changing experience, but maybe it was all it could be to a 12-year-old. I'd been raised in a Christian home with Christian values, but by the time I was old enough to be on my own, I had no problem with doing my own thing. I ran with the crowd, too busy to attend church. I didn't exactly turn my back on God; I just didn't take the time to be His. I was more interested in making excuses rather than making commitments.

John suggested that I get re-baptized to rededicate my life to God and rekindle our lost relationship. John was right. What had I been doing all these years? It was so clear to me what a dangerous game I'd been playing, not just with my physical life, but also with my eternal life. It was a game that I couldn't afford to lose.

I didn't want to wait until I was finally home to be baptized in my own church. I knew our minister, Burt Brock, was due for a visit in a few days, and with my new sense of urgency, plans were made for my new baptism in the therapy pool. To the best of my knowledge, a pool baptism had never happened at RHI.

This kind of a baptism was a first for everybody involved, including Burt. It was an exciting day, but it was hard not to be nervous as a mini-crane lowered me into the pool and Burt's inexperienced arms. A therapist joined us in the water, watching carefully in case of emergency. Burt had performed hundreds of baptisms, but this was his first with someone who was paralyzed. If he dropped me, I could *really* drown, making us the lead story on the 10 o'clock news. Imagine the headline, "Quadriplegic drowned by pastor, film at 10."

This time around, my baptism was monumental to my life. It was everything it should have been the first time. When golfers hit a ball in the wrong direction they get to take what is called a mulligan (a do-over). I considered that day my mulligan and I was more than eager to start over.

***

As I felt my relationship with God growing stronger every day, the need to honor Him in a Christian setting with fellow believers tugged at me. A small room served as a chapel for RHI patients on Sunday mornings, and Mom agreed to attend with me for the first time. We were surprised, considering the sheer number of patient residents at RHI, how few actually made the effort to attend. Of course, many couldn't attend due to their condition, but were the rest of them just too angry and blaming God for what had happened to them?

I really missed my minister, Burt, and his wonderful uplifting messages, but I was eager to hear the message by the visiting volunteer minister and to be inspired by a powerful sermon. News flash: all ministers are not created equal. We were huddled together in the tiny chapel, tight with patients in wheelchairs. The minister appeared to be in his mid-70s, possibly even older. He started out by assuring all of us patients that he could relate to our situation. He informed us that he, too, had suffered a devastating injury.

I remember thinking how wonderful it was that he was here to encourage us with his own story of recovery. All ears were eagerly tuned to hear the account of his life and death experience.

It caught me by surprise when he started by telling us that his accident had happened in the kitchen. Who experiences life and death in the kitchen? Well, apparently he did. The old pastor held up his hand for us to clearly see as he proceeded to explain how he'd cut his tendon near his thumb and required a visit to the emergency room and stitches to repair the damage. He related how he had suffered with this trauma by giving a blow-by-blow description of his recovery, which qualified him to understand what we were going through. By this time Mom was about to fall off her chair laughing and I thought to myself, *he must be kidding; this is no time for jokes.* Then I realized that he was dead serious.

My experience at chapel that Sunday morning helped enlighten me as to why so few attended. Maybe God was being merciful. Bless the pastor's effort, but I just couldn't bring myself to go back. Thankfully, three members of my own congregation, Lee Eckart, Ed Neff, and Rex Edwards, came every Sunday to bring devotion and share communion with me. They would drive an hour each way plus the time they spent with me, and I really appreciated that. They were giving up their own family time for me. It truly was a service of God, the Body of Christ in motion.

※※※※※※※※※※※※※※※※※※※※※※※

The Bible says that *a cheerful heart is good medicine* (Proverbs 17:22). Laughter was oftentimes what kept the staff and patients going, and I think the nurses especially looked for opportunities to have fun.

Student nurses from the local colleges appeared on a weekly basis. Fortunately, we patients weren't subjected to being their guinea pigs until we had become more or less veterans. Fresh from nursing school, young 20-something girls, timid, shy, and not yet comfortable with patient care, would show up for their tour of duty. These student nurses were assigned to a seasoned nurse who would assist in giving them the full nursing experience, and they probably

A Mission of Faith

got more than they bargained for. I'm sure they thought they would be doing nothing more than taking temperatures and passing out aspirins. Wrong!

Each time I was formally introduced to the newest "kid nurse," which was my term of endearment for each of these yet uninitiated young women, she would shyly say, "Hello, Mr. Woods, so nice to meet you." I smiled because I knew what was coming. As I responded, "I hope you have warm hands," an uncomprehending look flashed across her face as the veteran nurse would order, "Would you please catheterize Mr. Woods?" Without sounding too insensitive, the look of sheer terror was comical; after all, we had just met. This scenario played out over and over during my stay at RHI and it was as funny the first time as it was the last. I hope I was never responsible for any career changes. As I said earlier, I'd found it much easier to cope at RHI by checking my dignity at the door. I hoped I'd remember to pick it back up when it would be time to return home.

One day, while kid-nurse for the day and I were preparing my home field for this uncomfortable and embarrassing procedure, she draped me with a sterile paper covering. Then she punched a hole in the center of the paper and pulled my team captain through the hole, ready for catheterization. I couldn't stop myself from blurting, "Hey, a puppet show!" It broke the ice; all seriousness and embarrassment were gone as we both laughed 'til we cried. I'm sure "veteran nurse" spread the details of the incident all over the wing.

At this stage of my therapy, the dexterity and movement in my hands was minimal. But because I could now move my left shoulder forward and back, I was able to utilize this newly acquired motion to drive a power wheelchair with a joystick. This was a monumental step forward, my first taste of independence. I still needed to be placed in the chair, strapped in, and my paralyzed hand lifted and set onto the joystick, which resembled a mini-football goal, so it wouldn't slip off.

99

At first this was a shaky learning experience, as a few wall cracks and chipped paint will attest. But I quickly mastered the skill and soon people were clearing the halls when I raced to the gym. Like deer in the headlights of an oncoming vehicle, they hugged the walls as I whizzed by. I would be lying if I said I didn't get a kick out of seeing them scramble out of my way. There were times I even pretended to be more out of control than I actually was, just to watch them jump. Anything to entertain myself.

Several weeks into my therapy program, the emphasis shifted to working on being able to transfer myself in and out of my wheelchair. I wasn't sure how this was going to happen, but I was tired of having other people lifting me out of bed and plopping me into my chair like a sack of potatoes. My fear was always that they might drop me, causing further injury, and I sure didn't need that.

As each week went by, it was becoming easier for me to visualize an independent life; maybe not normal, but functional nonetheless. It didn't matter to me if the tasks I was performing were pretty or not, just if it worked. I was gaining more strength and control in my hands and arms, with my left side being the strongest. My gym rat days kicked in full force and I was ready to do whatever it took to get through each day. Leave tomorrow's worries where they belonged, in tomorrow. After all, the Bible says *do not worry about tomorrow, for tomorrow will worry about itself. Each day has enough trouble of its own* (Matthew 6:34). I could only concentrate on today and I would give it all I had, tomorrow would be its own day. I was careful not to look too far ahead, knowing that the monumental amount of work to come might be discouraging. Winning the war was the whole picture, but the battles were fought daily.

There were times when Amy would leave me unattended with instructions to do 10 repetitions of a particular exercise. I wanted to push myself, surpassing her goal of 10 to do 20, maybe even 30 reps.

In my mind, standard reps were going to produce standard results; I wasn't interested in standard results. The old saying "If you do what everyone else does then you'll get what everyone else gets" had more meaning now than ever before. When I'd see Amy returning, I would start counting off 461, 462, 463 just to elicit a laugh from her. Her response was a smirk and, "Yeah, right!" Amy took her job very seriously, but she had a light-hearted approach to her patients, peppered generously with a biting sense of humor. We blended well together.

At times a group of us patients would be placed in a circle with one-pound weights strapped into our hands (because we had no gripping ability) with instructions to do curls. At first it was futile. There was no way I could begin to lift something so heavy. A one-pound weight, which may as well have been a ton, just hung in my limp hand as I struggled to raise it even an inch. Before the crash I had curled 50-pound dumbbells and bench-pressed 300 pounds. Now, even one pound was beyond my capability. All my limbs felt like 100-pound weights had been permanently attached to each one. Imagine having that kind of weight attached to your hand and then trying to scratch your nose. My whole body, and each part of it, was unbelievably heavy to me and it took everything I had to make even the slightest movement. I would strain and grunt with the simplest tasks like I was trying to lift a car.

I knew the whole gym could hear me struggling, but I didn't care, I was there to work. As I looked around, other patients were also grimacing and struggling with their own heaviness. The majority of patients took their work to heart, with a few exceptions. The most obvious one to me was a young single mother who complained about being awakened so early to start her day in therapy. When I heard her say, "I want to sleep in until 10:00 a.m.," I couldn't believe it. This was to be her life and she wasn't taking her therapy serious at all. She only had a small window of opportunity at RHI, which would dictate the outcome for the rest of her life. She wasn't grasping the importance of therapy. This was not the time or place to be lazy.

>>>>>>>>>>>>>>>>>>>>>>>>>>>>>>>>>>>>>>
>>>>>>>>>>>>>>>>>>>>>>>>>>>>>>>>>>>>>>
>>>>>>>>>>>>>>>>>>>>>>>>>>>>>>>>>>>

Throughout my life, I hadn't given my body any real credit for all the work it did, performing the smallest tasks. Our muscle structure responds to our brain signals directing us to move our body parts. My brain signal had been short-circuited and even the strongest muscle, without that signal, was useless. The body truly is a real piece of God's engineering at its best.

While my body wasn't cooperating, at least my mind was. I could look around the therapy gym and see head trauma patients whose injuries resulted from accidents or strokes. Some of these patients were only physically present, unable to mentally understand or respond to therapy instructions. My heart went out especially to their family members, who were now dealing with the nightmare of losing a loved one. Not through death like at a funeral, but worse, their loved one was gone but the body was still living. No matter the situation, the families still dealt with it with strength, courage, and grace. All of the families were sustained by the hope of recovery. They didn't cry; they just showed up every day giving support, love, and encouragement. I'm sure the tears that were left at the door when they entered RHI were picked up again as they returned home.

In a patient's mind, the goal is complete recovery as if the life-altering incident never happened. In the therapist's mind, recovery is defined differently. From their perspective, recovery is being able to function on your own in life, being able to live independently with minimal outside assistance. Learning to perform simple tasks was critical, tasks like putting on your own socks, brushing your teeth, sticking a spoon in your mouth, removing lids, or picking up objects. Being able to touch fingers to thumb (pinching) is a huge step toward independent living. Without this ability, a patient can't pick up anything. I had never before realized the importance of being able to pinch my fingers together. Few people experience this disability, at least not on a permanent level. Broken fingers heal quickly and the inconvenience is soon forgotten.

Looking around the gym I could see patients relearning many of the routine tasks that most people take for granted. Some patients were learning to navigate a mock kitchen, bathroom, shower, or car. The average person would consider getting in and out of a car a basic task; even a two-year-old can do it. But try doing one of these simple tasks when your body feels like it weighs a thousand pounds.

In the mock kitchen I joined a group of a half-dozen patients. Our therapy assignment was to make chocolate chip cookies. Those who were *only* paralyzed from the waist down at least had use of their hands and just needed to navigate their wheelchair into position while leaving the cabinets intact. The quadriplegics were a totally different story. Imagine trying to crack an egg while wearing two hundred pound boxing gloves, because that's just what it felt like. Even though we managed to get the cookies made, I wanted to shout across the gym, "Clean up on aisle three." What a mess!

We felt like we were the Martha Stewarts of RHI. The staff was to bake the cookies over lunchtime, and that afternoon we were to return and take them for a taste drive. I thought I'd have to go postal on someone when I found out they had all been eaten by the time I returned. My favorite cookies that I'd struggled so hard to make—all gone! Note to self: don't be late for cookie tasting.

Fortunately, the bathroom therapy wasn't a group activity. I guess the therapists realized that a room full of strangers circling one poor schmuck sitting on the stool wasn't beneficial to anyone's self-esteem. The purpose of bathroom therapy was to learn to transfer your assets from the chair to the throne on your own. This was a trickier procedure than you can imagine. One false move could put me with my head in the head. After some concentrated therapy, Amy told me I was now ready to go on my own, but still being catheterized, I wasn't yet on my own.

While in the bathroom, we also practiced transfer from wheelchair to tub/shower combination. This was a lot more involved than a toilet transfer. At some point in time, I was looking forward to being able to shower myself. I wasn't sure when that day would come, but I was hopeful. Imagine having to be showered by a total stranger, your mother, or your wife (well okay, the wife thing was kind of cool), but you get the picture.

Even though my goal when I entered therapy was to walk again, RHI's original focus was helping me learn to feed myself. This basic life need is so underestimated by most of us, so taken for granted that it doesn't even cross our minds. I wanted to be able to sit at the dining room table and not be fed by my wife or kids. Thankfully, after weeks of therapy, I had gained enough strength and dexterity in my left hand and fingers to at least get food into my mouth without help. Getting to this point was gigantic, a mental milestone, just short of walking in my goal book.

Proudly, I rang the therapy bell that day, or maybe I should say the dinner bell.

9
My Wife, the Trooper

My constant through all this was my wife, Tina. After a hard day of therapy, I would lay in my bed exhausted, but ready for Tina's company. She always brightened my day then as she does now.

We tried not to dwell on the negative aspects of our life. I knew she had worries and stress as she dealt with the home front, the twins, and a job, but they didn't show on her face when she came into my room. Her worries were somewhat alleviated by my mom living at our house during this time. Mom covered a lot of the daily tasks and babysitting for the twins while Tina worked, which allowed her to spend evenings with me.

Knowing that the kids were in good hands with Grandma, Tina would curl up with me in the hospital bed, and it was so comforting just having her there beside me. Our conversations were always the typical husband-wife exchange: "How was your day?" "What did you do today?" She would tell me how her work had gone that day and I'd tell her proudly, "I fed myself some Jell-o today." Well, maybe not the usual husband-wife exchange, but our version of it.

By the time visiting hours were over, I would be falling asleep. I was tired and so relaxed by having her there that I would invariably be nodding off by the time she had to go. I didn't want to see her leave, but I also needed the sleep. Another big day of therapy would begin early the next morning. We each had a job to do and we both took them seriously.

Because I was so totally focused on my recovery, I wasn't always aware of what Tina, the kids, and my extended family were experiencing. Tina cried over the phone when I called her from West Virginia to tell her about the crash. She later told me that she still cried, but made it a point to never do it in front of the kids or me.

During my time at RHI, Tina was working full time, trying to spend time with the kids, and after work spending time with me also. The drive to RHI was a two hour round trip from our house, so she usually didn't get home at night until 10:30. My mother would already have the kids in bed asleep, and Tina would give them a kiss then go to bed herself, having to be back at work early the next morning. When she wanted to spend an evening with the kids, my mother would come up to visit me. Tina kept this grueling schedule for nearly two months, and although it must have been exhausting, she never complained. My angel, the trooper.

I was making progress, albeit it slowly. After enduring weeks of discomfort, the hard plastic neck brace that I'd been wearing was finally removed. It felt so good to be free of that contraption, even though I was still experiencing severe neck pain. I was assured that this kind of pain was to be expected after such a traumatic injury, and that it would subside with time. The staff at RHI wasn't overly concerned about the pain since they considered it par for the course,

...le another X-ray on my neck was performed the day ...ving. They told me they wouldn't have the results back ...ay.

..., to boost my morale, I was allowed to go home for a ...ugh on Thanksgiving Day. I was so excited to be able ...nd spend holiday time with my family. I hadn't been in ...le since before the accident, and although I was looking ...ing there, things were going to be different. Now I would ...gate the rooms in a wheelchair. Was this going to be my ...way of life? Maybe so, but right now, I was thrilled to be ...e.

...d and Uncle Howard picked me up at RHI. It seemed ...d a little scary just being in a car that was traveling fast ...highway. For over a month the only speed I'd experienced ...I was wheeling down the hall. In the car, it felt like I ...g as scenery whizzed by me and my body tried to adjust ...rception of what normal speed was. Thirty miles an hour ...y felt like a hundred.

...n we pulled into the driveway an hour later, everything ...new and different somehow. It was fall when I'd left for ...irginia, now winter was beginning to set in. Dad pulled ...eelchair from the trunk and then he and my Uncle Howard ...d me into it. Tina had cooked a standard Thanksgiving ...with all the fixings, and I caught the aroma of the roasting ...before we even entered the house. RHI had good food, but ...n't home cooking.

...ad and Uncle Howard helped me into my favorite recliner so ...uld watch some of the football game while Tina and Mom ...red dinner. I enjoyed watching Bailey and Bryce run and play, ...especially loved it when they climbed in and out of the recliner ...me. I wanted to put my arms around them and hug them, but I couldn't. Finally, I was back at home again with my family and everything seemed normal. Other than me being paralyzed and in a wheelchair.

I sensed Tina's uneasiness about what our future held and I'd be lying if I said I didn't question that myself. I wondered if this house was going to continue to be our home. Financially, would we be able to keep the new house we had planned so carefully and worked so hard to build? It was hard to imagine being able to work again in this condition.

At that point, everything was so uncertain. I was beginning to understand that things are just things, but this was our home and relocating the kids and us would be, in my condition, a major undertaking. I tried hard to block all these worries from my mind at least for the day as I settled in to enjoy my family and just being with them. At that stage in my life, the material things that I had valued so much suddenly took a back seat to what was *really* important in life.

Before the accident, I wasn't any different than most people who enmesh themselves in cars, houses, jobs, and success. To fit into society's thinking, you had to buy into the mentality of the importance of *stuff*. Well, stuff wasn't turning the wheels on my wheelchair. Stuff wasn't moving my legs or hands or helping me work hard in therapy. What was stuff really good for, anyway? Did it make me or anyone else feel better about ourselves? Did it help me fit in or draw respect from my friends and family? Did it light up my kids' faces or make my wife love me more? No! These truths became abundantly clear in the mountains of West Virginia.

It was a wonderful Thanksgiving celebration, which brought me an amazing sense of normalcy, but the hours flew by far too quickly and it was time to return to RHI. The kids didn't want me to go; they couldn't understand why I had to leave. I didn't want to go, either.

Wheelchair or not, I wanted to stay home and be Daddy again. But I knew I still had work to do before staying home and being Daddy was a reality. It was so sad and heart wrenching to look back over my shoulder at my family as I left to return to RHI. If I was to have a chance at all for any type of recovery, returning to RHI's therapy gym was a must—even though some referred to it as the torture chamber.

I had only been back at RHI for an hour, still pumped up over my visit home, when a nurse rushed into my room with a neck brace in her hand. "Don't move! Don't move!" she said sternly. I was startled. What was she saying? What was going on? Why the neck brace?

I could see the fear in her eyes as she said, "Mr. Woods, your X-ray results just came in." She paused a moment before adding, "You've had a broken neck since you got here."

At first I couldn't comprehend what I was hearing. The thought processed slowly in my mind. A broken neck? What did that mean at this point in time? I thought of all the straining and struggling that I'd been doing in therapy, and now they're telling me that all the while my neck was broken? What about the manipulation the therapist had done to my body? My Lord, are you kidding me?

In one split second, my wonderful high from being home with my family was gone and I was back in the pit of hell. It was like being sucker punched in the gut. A month and a half's worth of work was down the drain and I had just returned to ground zero. Only moments earlier I had been so uplifted and ready for battle. Was this Satan's way of dragging me back down once again? Was he trying to break my spirit by stealing everything I'd worked so hard to build?

First thing the next morning I was to be taken by ambulance back to Methodist Hospital for a CT scan. It was an unbelievably long night. With the neck brace back in place, I was terrified of moving, almost afraid to breathe for fear of severing my spinal cord. What if I fell asleep and unintentionally moved the wrong way, doing more irreversible damage? It was a night of horror. In the darkest hours I faced the ramifications of what all this meant to me and to my recovery.

I didn't know if I had the strength to start all over again. That thought kept my mind racing all night as sleep eluded me, until, that is, I remembered the words of Jesus that I'd recently read. *The thief comes only to steal and kill and destroy; I have come that they may have life, and have it to the full* (John 10:10). I decided that I was not going to let Satan steal what God had already given to me: His word that I was going to be okay. I decided that if I wasn't going to be able to sleep that night, I would occupy my mind with the phrase that had continued to empower me since the moment I first said it: I can do *anything* through Christ who strengthens me.

I was anxious for answers the next morning when the paramedics arrived to take me back to Methodist Hospital. By now I hadn't slept for over 24 hours. I was exhausted from my trip home followed by this turn of events. My dad followed the ambulance to Methodist to be whatever support he could.

It was the usual hurry up and wait scenario again at Methodist. It seemed like forever for the scan to be completed and the results confirmed. When the doctor finally entered the room, my heart began to race as I mentally prepared myself for the worst. What was he going to tell me? How bad was it?

"False alarm," the doctor said, almost nonchalantly. "It was only a shadow on the X-ray that didn't mean anything."

I was stunned as I sat there silent, for what seemed like a full minute. I could feel my face getting hot as I was grinding my teeth. I wanted to scream. Did they have any clue what they had just put me through? My future hung on a *shadow*? Despite all of my conflicting feelings, I was elated. No broken neck. Therapy could resume without fear of damage. No setback.

As it turned out, I was able to use this ordeal as a catalyst of strength, a real motivator for weeks to come. I returned to RHI with a renewed determination. I would win, whatever win meant in my recovery book.

The RHI staff shared my elation, apologizing profusely for having put me through this ordeal as they took back the hated neck brace. Let the games begin—again.

Tina's sister Anita came in from Missouri late that Friday. Every year Tina and Anita went shopping after Thanksgiving, kicking off the Christmas rush. Tina was in desperate need of the down time from all the stress she was under, and I was glad she could get away to spend a few happy hours with her sister. Tina needed to forget RHI, therapy, my physical limitations, her job, arrangements for the kids, and our uncertain future, if only for a few hours. She had a myriad of issues to deal with on a daily basis.

On their way home from shopping, Tina and Anita stopped by to see me at RHI, where I met them in the lobby in my power wheelchair. Tina looked more relaxed and happy than I had seen her since the crash. Anita was a different story. I could see shock and genuine concern that registered on her face. After all, this was the first time she had seen me like this, and all the explaining in the world done over the phone couldn't replace seeing it in person.

I did my best to lighten the mood by inquiring about family back home and keeping the conversation upbeat. They'd had a great day together, and I didn't want to be the catalyst for ending it with gloom and doom. I still wasn't sure what the future held, but I reassured my sister-in-law that everything would be fine. I wanted Anita to go back to Missouri with a positive report on my condition, even though I wasn't sure I was being completely honest with her. We said our good-byes late that afternoon, and I returned to my wing to prepare for dinner.

During the day, therapy times varied for patients, and meals did also. But dinnertime was different; we usually ate together in the lobby area of the spinal cord wing. This was therapeutic for us all, new and old patients alike. Dining together allowed us to exchange progress reports, offer encouragement, and discuss issues only we could understand. Although the ages of those at the table varied from 16 to 65 years, neither age, nor gender or race mattered; we were all on an equal playing field. We were all seated at the same table, but how we came to be there was each individual's story. New patients always meant new stories.

A pretty young cheerleader involved in a bus accident had been paralyzed from the waist down. That was tragic enough, but two others on her bus were killed.

A banker who went deer hunting had fallen out of his deer stand, leaving him paralyzed from the neck down.

A 16-year-old boy had been paralyzed from the waist down for the past two years; simple fun turned tragic while he was wrestling with his father. They both slipped on the kitchen floor. Their lives would never be the same again. As a father myself, I can't imagine the guilt his dad must have felt. There were times when the boy seemed bitter. At first I thought this was terribly sad, but thinking back to when I was his age, how devastating it would have been. It was tragic enough for me at 39 years old, but I had already experienced a pretty full life. On the other hand, he was just getting started.

That kid still had a wild streak in him because he always wanted to race our power wheelchairs down the hallway. After spending a lifetime trying to fulfill my own need for speed, now all of a sudden I was actually afraid of a simple drag race through the hospital. After all, I could get hurt. Since I was old enough to be his father, I thought it only proper that I set a good example and refuse to race. But when he called me a chicken it was game on.

I blew his doors off.

When the fun and games were over, it was back to the therapy gym where there was an unusual treadmill near a window. There was some sort of harness contraption hanging over it, but I honestly didn't know what it was for and had not seen anyone use it. Now it was my turn to give it a try. I was either going to be successful or swing like Peter Pan from that harness.

It took four therapists to hook me up and then an electric motor hoisted me from my chair and suspended me over the treadmill. One therapist controlled the treadmill speed, one steadied me, and a therapist was assigned to each foot.

When they first started the treadmill moving, my feet just drug across it. I thought to myself, *boy this is no help*. It was a fairly new piece of equipment and I suspect the therapists were learning right along with me. The therapists on each foot grabbed my shoestrings and told me to flex my legs like I would if I were walking. As I tried to flex, they would lift each foot in stride planting it firmly back onto the treadmill surface as I mimicked walking. I figured this was intended to trick the brain into believing the body was walking. I knew the therapists were doing 99.9% of the work, but it did kind of feel like I was walking and it felt great.

Out of all the things that I did at RHI, accomplishing this task was monumental, head and shoulders above everything else. I believed that this was the turning point that would eventually enable me to walk again. I'm not embarrassed to admit that I cried that day when I rang that therapy bell as loudly as I possibly could. That entire gym knew that G.L. Woods had walked that day. I could hardly wait to get back to my room and call Tina to share this fantastic news with her. I felt like I had been to the edge, looked over into the abyss, and was now slowly backing away from it...on my own two feet.

From then on, I eagerly looked forward to what I called "treadmill time." I knew it unlocked the door to my walking alone. My legs would now start to awaken as one step would lead to two, and I would build on this foundation for weeks to come. This was a tedious process, testing my patience. I was ready to run, but my sleepy legs were taking their time. Eventually the heaviness in my legs began to lighten up and the thousand pound legs started to feel like eight hundred pounds, then six hundred, and on down as I progressed.

It was hard to believe that when I'd entered RHI just six weeks earlier, I was totally paralyzed from the neck down. Now I was actually upright again, and my limbs were being retrained to walk. They say that one word from God can change your life forever, and I fully believed that I was truly going to be okay—regardless of what the final outcome looked like.

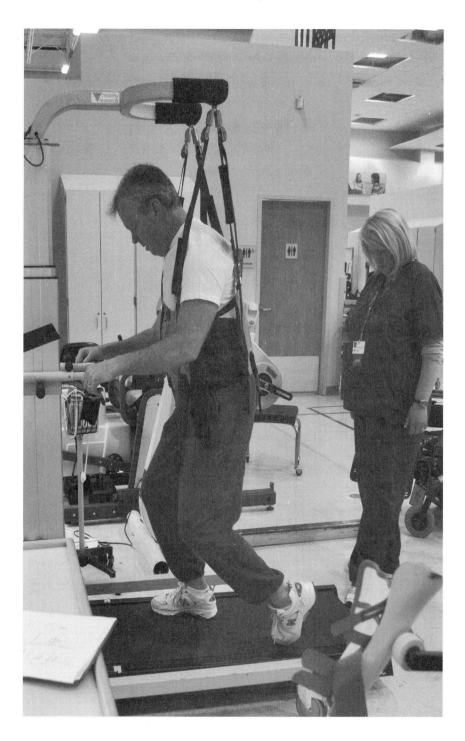

10

Therapists, Meet Mr. Thong

On the back of my wheelchair was a backpack where all my therapy and personal supplies were kept, including a swimsuit that would be used for my new therapy in the swimming pool. I was very excited about it. Working in the pool would be something different, a tool to help me learn to fight gravity, and I was ready to start. I was to show up at the gym fully dressed, and some woman would then have to strip me down and get my swimsuit on me. By now the list of staff that was *familiar* with me was so long that I'd stopped counting.

When I arrived at the pool for my first day of therapy, excitement turned to terror when it hit me, *wait a minute, I'm not a swimmer anymore and I could drown.* Like the old kid's joke, "What do you call a man in a pool with no arms and no legs?—Bob," that's just how I felt. A small crane was attached to a chase-type lounge, which was then lowered with me in it, into the water. My therapist was waiting for me in the pool as I thought to myself, *this is really a dumb idea.*

Little, petite Leslie was the only thing that stood between me and getting my lungs full of water. She was also the only one in that pool who had any confidence. I knew that Leslie wasn't going to drown

119

me on purpose, but what if, like Amy, she looked away for a minute and I slowly sank to the bottom of the pool? I began to take a mental inventory. How nice had I really been to Leslie during the previous week? Had I said anything mean to her? Maybe this was all her master plan in the name of therapy. She would tell the police, "It was just a terrible therapy accident," and no jail time for her.

Leslie placed her arms under my body and encouraged me to try to float. She looked me dead in the face, knowing my terror, and reassured me that she would take care of me. I had no other choice but to take her at her word. Even though the first session that day was unsettling, I eventually learned to love pool therapy. In the coming weeks I worked on the submerged parallel bars. My buoyancy in the water allowed my limbs to move easier without fighting gravity and my actual weight. This pool therapy would prove to be pivotal to my recovery.

No part of RHI was insulated against the jokester, pool therapy included. I was willing to do whatever it took to get a laugh (the best medicine). I told one of my church friends that I was involved in pool therapy each week and joked, "I wonder what they would do if I wore a thong swimsuit?" The following week my friends came to visit, wielding the most hideous leopard skin thong, complete with dangling tassels. I was thrilled. Into my wheelchair bag it went. I couldn't wait for the next pool therapy day and my big unveiling. When the day finally arrived, I could hardly keep a straight face as I sped to my pool session.

Vicki, a therapist assistant, would be my first victim. She was a sweet 50-ish African-American lady. "Hey Vicki, would you mind helping me into my swimsuit?"

She cordially responded, "Of course, sweetheart."

I watched as she rummaged through my bag looking for the elusive suit. She began stammering, trying to figure out what she'd gotten hold of as she dragged that hideous thong from my supply bag, tassels swaying. "What the hell?" was all she could get out before she caught the joke. "You ornery thing!" she exclaimed. I was laughing hysterically, and she was too, before her light bulb came on and she said, "Wait right here. I want to get Amy."

Vicki coaxed Amy over to handle swimsuit detail as she scurried around the corner so she could hide and watch the fun. One by one, at least half a dozen helpers were recruited to assist Mr. Woods with his suit that day. Fun was fun in any form, and Mr. Thong got a lot of mileage. I never actually wore it in the pool for fear of *rope burn*, even though the staff double-dog dared me.

When I wasn't in the pool, I would periodically take notice of a therapist working with a stroke or brain injury patient on the parallel bars in the gym. It was hard for me to imagine ever progressing to that point. I had used parallel bars in pool therapy, but there the water had supported my weight. Those sessions went pretty well, if you don't count the couple of near death drowning experiences. However, supporting my own body outside the pool with arms that felt like overcooked noodles was a whole different ballgame. But after more than a month at RHI, I was given a shot at testing my fortitude and strength on the parallel bars.

It felt so foreign and bizarre. My control was out-of-control. I was a wobbly mass of Jell-o as I tried to stand on legs that weren't mine and certainly weren't responding to my mental commands. My instructions were to pull my wheelchair up to the bars, lean forward to the point of almost falling out, then grab the bars and try to stand.

I had several false starts at first. I would get halfway up, then arms and legs would give out and I'd flop backward into the chair. I did this over and over again. I was beginning to think I would never accomplish the assignment. I just didn't have it in me to get out of that chair. The spirit was willing, but the body wasn't convinced yet.

The therapist kept encouraging me to try again, just one more time. Finally, with a frail grasp on the bars and the therapist's support, I was heaved upward onto my feet. Trying to keep my balance caused my whole body to tremble and shake with the effort. It took everything I had in me to stand for the first time. But I was excited; I was actually standing. Just standing for a few seconds was totally and completely exhausting, but it was worth the effort.

I felt like I had just finished a three-hour workout. It was weird; I was used to seeing the gym at a 48-inch level from my wheelchair. Now, for the first time, I surveyed the room from my full six-foot height, a whole new perspective. Until then I hadn't known if standing or walking would ever happen, but I was starting to see a light at the end of my dark tunnel. Would I really be able to walk?

I knew that I wanted to continue to fight for this dream and see how far I could go with it. I think my therapists were genuinely shocked that I had succeeded, but they were as thrilled as I was. Now that I'd proved I could stand, therapy intensified in this area as I built upon my successes. I had reached a real milestone, and once again the bell was ringing for me.

I had finally recovered to the point of being able to stand by myself. It was awesome just being able to stand up from my wheelchair. Even though I wasn't walking, it was still an exciting accomplishment.

When it came time for my next occupational therapy session, Amy had been off for a few days and she wasn't aware that I was standing on my own now. My brother John was visiting at the time and I couldn't wait for the two of us to get to the gym after lunch so I could show off my new skill. I was anxious to see Amy's reaction. She was talking to other staff members when John and I approached her. I knew it was rude to interrupt, but I couldn't wait any longer. I just knew she would be as excited as I was.

I told my brother, "Wait 'til you see the look on Amy's face," then

I said, "Hey Amy, what do you think about this?"

I cautiously stood up from my chair, watching the expression on Amy's face turn from wonder, to delight…and then to shock. For a split second I didn't understand her reaction, until my brother casually said, "Hey dude, your pants fell down."

They say that what goes up must come down, and I was exposed as Mother Nature had made me, with my pants pooled around my ankles. Oh yeah, did I mention I wasn't wearing underwear that day?

I could only stand there motionless, in full view of Amy and everyone else, not being able to bend over to retrieve my pants. My supportive brother was laughing so hard that he was no help either. Amy kept her cool and just drawled "nice" as she gave me a thumbs up.

Apparently, what goes around comes around, because "kid-nurse" had failed to tie the drawstring on my sweatpants after the catheterization back in my room. Did I say that the list of those who had become "familiar" with me was long? Well, it just got a lot longer. Unfortunately, this incident made me an RHI legend, and years later they are still laughing about it. To my friends at RHI: glad I could be of service.

Things started to move faster as my confession that I can do *anything* through Christ who strengthens me became reality. I was totally convinced that if I could stand, then I could also take steps. I was right, because eventually I graduated to a tall-wheeled walker with padded arm supports and upright grips. At first all I could manage was only a few steps, but that earned me the right to ring the therapy bell. I started walking a little farther and farther each day, ringing the bell with each passing session. Each time the bell rang, the cheers in the gym got louder and louder. The looks of doubt that I'd once received were now transformed into warm smiles of victory, as if to say, "He's done it – he's actually done it!"

Even though my wheelchair remained my primary mode of

transportation, I knew the day was coming when I would be able to walk on my own and leave that chair behind me forever.

I was nearing the end of my time at RHI. I would soon be leaving for home and the staff was trying to prepare me for that transition. Not that I was totally leaving RHI, because I would still return for additional therapy as an outpatient. Two months in a hospital setting is a long time, but my stay had been so filled with recovery activities that the weeks had flown by. I was anxious to sleep in my own bed, to have dinner with my family, and to return to a normal life. Well, as normal as it could be after the accident.

I had been through Logan Hospital and all they could do, then Huntington Hospital and all they could do, then Methodist Hospital and all they could do. As I went home from RHI I wondered, was everything I experienced all *they* could do? This would be the end of the hospital line; home was the final stop and any additional recovery would depend on my body and me. I questioned how much more recovery God would allow me to achieve.

Part of the departing process at RHI included a visit with the in-house psychiatrist. I had never been to one and wasn't sure if lying on the couch or talking about my childhood were prerequisites. I think the doctor expected me to be depressed and beaten down. I'm sure he had seen these scenarios played out before. He talked about the hard life I was now facing and asked what were my feelings on that. How was my support system at home? When I had broken my leg before the twins were born, I had jokingly nicknamed Tina "Miss Compassion." That thought now humorously flashed across my mind. In all seriousness, I knew my support system was rock solid and I told him so.

As we continued our conversation, his prompting statements

seemed to imply that with all that had happened, I had every right to feel depressed and sorry for myself. That's when I stopped him in mid-sentence, "Dude you have no idea how happy I am with how this has turned out for me. I feel like I've been to the edge and back and I'm thrilled to be going home. My goal when I came to RHI was to leave here on my feet and I *will* walk out of here!"

As far as I was concerned it didn't get any better than that. I was so excited about going home that I could hardly live with myself. This was a new ballgame for me, a life totally different from what it had been before. My focus has shifted dramatically. Life was *gooooood!*

"Congratulations," he said, "it sounds like you don't need me. You have it under control." He wished me luck as I wheeled out of his office.

I could see the proverbial light at the end of the tunnel. Even though the thought of going home was exciting, I was also leaving the very real security of RHI. They had done their part, all they could, and like a kid going off to college, the "folks" were cutting me loose. But for them, other kids would fill my place at RHI.

It was scary knowing that they had done all they could. I wasn't going on to another hospital or rehab facility. Those days were behind me; all the stops were done. My last stop would be *my* home, thank God, not a nursing home, which, sadly, happens in some cases. My last 24 hours were filled with goodbyes, support for my success, well wishes, and requests to "Come back and see us."

I had endured being catheterized six to eight times a day throughout my entire stay at RHI, and the nurses had gently encouraged Tina to learn the process. When I went home, she would need to catheterize me, because without hand dexterity I was unable to do this for myself. Tina kept putting them off, I think hoping that before that day arrived I would be going on my own. I'm convinced that she spoke desperately to God about this because the day before I left RHI, the floodgates were opened and nature took its course. I was as proud as a two-year-old going potty for the first time, and I'm sure Tina mentally wiped her brow in relief. Hallelujah! A close call for both of us.

Another part of RHI's exit strategy was to transition us back into a normal home life. My last night would be spent with Tina in a little mock apartment setting down the hall from my room. Our RHI home had a kitchen, a living room, a bedroom, and a bath, which allowed us a practice run of what home life would be like while still having my RHI safety net in place. The staff would be there to assist with any unexpected problems we might experience.

I had practiced transferring to and from my wheelchair many times in therapy, but I still wasn't comfortable doing it on my own. In that little apartment Tina and I ran through the routine of transferring me from wheelchair to bed, toilet, couch, then reversing the procedure and helping me get back into my wheelchair. The experiences we shared that night were firsts for both of us, and it was a bit unsettling. I wasn't used to needing her help so badly and she wasn't used to my dependency. Fortunately for me, although Tina is a petite girl, she is also very strong. I used to kiddingly tell my friends that when Tina and I would have an argument, I'd wanted to slug her sometimes—and I would have if I hadn't been so scared of her.

It was hard to relax and enjoy our time together that night. It was the first taste of our new life. The countdown had started and we would soon be living this scenario daily at home. Despite our apprehension, we had no issues and our apartment time went without a hitch.

The big day had arrived and it was time to go home. My nearly two months' stay at RHI was coming to a close. I remembered being whisked into that building in the fall of that year, flat on my back and staring at the ceiling, in the capable hands of paramedics who were rushing so to get onto their next assignment. Now winter had set in and I had come a long way in my recovery process.

Early on, with shaky bravado, I had told the staff, "I *will* walk out of here." Well, payday had arrived – cha-ching time! As I approached the front door in my wheelchair, which was being pushed by the staff member assigned to escort me to the car, I asked her to stop. I pulled on the manual brake lever, locking the chair in place, then I eased myself out of the chair. Then, aided by a walker, I proudly stepped through those doors to my waiting car. It wasn't a pretty sight, but I was walking and I felt wonderfully victorious. Thank you, God!

For with God nothing is ever impossible and no word from God shall be without power or impossible of fulfillment (Luke 1:38 AMP).

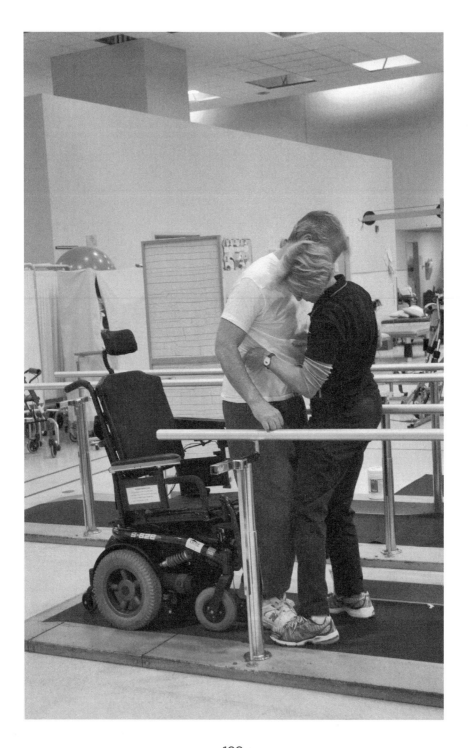

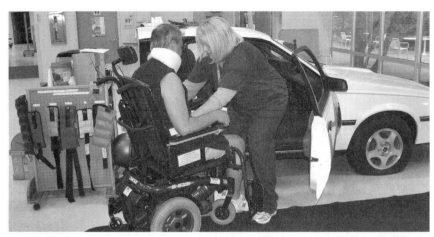

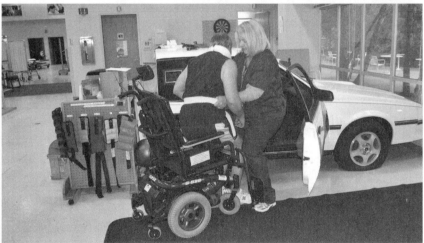

11

A New Beginning

After nearly two months of rehabilitation, I left RHI on a frigid December morning. Ozark National, the company I worked for, was having their Christmas sales meeting within 20 miles of RHI, and my buddy, Jude Hopper, had been vigorously encouraging me to make an appearance. "Everyone wants to see you," he said.

I didn't know if I was up to it physically or mentally. I wasn't sure I wanted to deal with the shock factor from those people who hadn't seen me, but had only heard about the accident and its aftermath. I reluctantly made the decision to go and when I arrived, just as I'd thought, there *was* that shock factor. After all, the last time most of these people had seen me I was a confident, energetic man. Now, as one of the ladies from the meeting kindly pointed out, "G.L., I've never seen you so frail." She wasn't trying to be mean; she just said the first thing that came to mind.

This scenario continued to play itself out over and over as I encountered people I knew, and who knew me, but hadn't seen me since my crash. I knew I'd have to face all these people over time: family, friends, clients, church members, and acquaintances. I expected that it would be awkward and uncomfortable at times as we struggled to carry on normal conversation. It's like going to a funeral and not knowing what to say.

I had been ordered to see my local physician within a week of returning home. RHI stressed the importance of keeping my family doctor informed of my current situation, but I wasn't sure why. I wasn't sick and RHI had done all they could for me, but I reluctantly called and made the appointment.

When the doctor came into the examining room and said, "What can I do for you?" I was taken back. I assumed that she'd seen my medical records that had been sent from RHI and was already fully aware of what had happened to me. As I began to explain to her what all had transpired since I last saw her, it was like telling the story to a ten-year-old. Her jaw kept dropping more and more as she exclaimed, "You've got to be kidding me!" I could tell she was stunned. I know she understood all that was meant by a C3 spinal injury, and found it difficult to comprehend a walking C3 patient.

She questioned me about all that had happened. In the end, she stressed the trauma of all I had been through and the upcoming holidays being a tough time of the year. I was caught off guard when she offered a Prozac prescription to help me cope. Now it was my turn, as my jaw dropped. How had she come to the conclusion that I was depressed? Is that how I came across to her? Was she getting a Prozac kickback? I felt like I had just weathered the perfect storm and now here was my doctor, getting ready to write me an anti-depressant prescription.

I started laughing. "Don't bother," I told her, I'm certainly *not* depressed. In fact I'm so excited about life right now that I could wet my pants." I think she got the picture.

In a short period of time I began experiencing a lot of firsts, meaning things that I hadn't dealt with in my previous life. For example, when I entered our church for the first time since the crash, a hush fell over the congregation as they turned to look at me, some shocked, some stunned, but most all with big smiles on their faces as they recognized God's miracle in me. Maybe they knew better than others the gravity of my injury because they had been kept up to speed from those church members and our minister, Burt Brock, who had regularly visited me at RHI.

It was good to be home. I no longer wanted to just occupy a seat in my church; I wanted to be involved in a serving ministry. I wanted to immerse myself in my church and become a real member of the flock, asking God to place me wherever my talents could best be utilized.

Before my crash, it was life before church. Now the excuse game wasn't going to fly anymore. My previous tour of duty on Sunday mornings consisted of riding the pew for an hour with an attitude of "don't bother me and maybe I'll be back next week." I was almost like a bride who, after the wedding ceremony, returns to her parent's home, telling her groom she will only see him for an hour each week and expects the relationship to survive. It's crazy to believe that offering God just one hour of our time each week could establish any sort of bond, but we use every excuse in the book to justify exactly that.

I hadn't been home long before friends and neighbors who hadn't been able to come to RHI started arriving for visits. Unlike at RHI, where visitors would be wielding the usual get well card or balloon, these new visitors were packin' chow. Hallelujah, dinner has arrived!

One special surprise visitor was my boss, Charlie Sharpe, who flew in from Missouri in the company's jet just to visit me. He was the CEO of the company and had a business to run, yet he took the time to come see how I was getting along. His genuine concern touched me deeply. He reassured me that I would continue to have a place in the organization as long as I wanted it. Over my career Charlie and I had developed a close relationship with many common interests, and it meant so much to me to have him there. We visited for several hours before he had to go back home. Since that time, we have become even closer, sharing a spiritual bond that is meaningful to both of us.

Tina, my mom, and I thought about taking the twins and going to Missouri for Christmas that year. Although we had lived in Indiana since the late 1980s, Missouri was still home to us and we had never missed a Christmas back home with family. But the weather turned bitterly cold, and as much as we wanted to go, wiser heads prevailed and we decided it was too risky. Things were different now; we could face a flat tire or breakdown and I would be of no help. My dad came to Indiana that year to spend Christmas with us. Even though it was different and out of the norm, it was a wonderful Christmas. I was in my own house, at least partial recovery was a reality, and the future held nothing but positive possibilities.

<hr/>

Before leaving RHI, I had been custom fitted with an orthopedic brace on my right leg to help stabilize my balance. It felt good to be home, and after a few weeks of practice in the house, I was more confident in my walking ability. The time had come to venture outside, and as soon as I was out the door I made a beeline for my man-cave, the garage, where as the comedian George Carlin would say, all my "stuff" was.

It had been months since I'd stepped through that door, where I now found a tiny time capsule of all that I had left undone before leaving the previous fall for my riding trip to West Virginia. I saw tools lying exactly where I had left them and projects in various stages of completion. I wondered if I would ever be able to pick up where I had left off. There were half-done welding jobs to be finished, and complicated fabrication work to be completed. There were also the usual man things: lawn mowers, weed-eaters, and leaf blowers, etc. As in most households, the unwritten rule generally is that the inside belongs to the wife and the husband takes care of the outside and the auto maintenance. But now, how was I going to hold up my end of the bargain? My mind still understood what needed to be done, but I would have to learn to use my new body in new and unfamiliar ways.

As I walked through the garage, taking inventory of all that still needed to be done someday, I struggled to envision how the various projects could or even would be completed. The old saying "If you want something done right, do it yourself," wasn't going to work for me. I would need the kind of help that I had never needed before. Most men understand that it's difficult admitting you need help. I would have to swallow my pride and accept the thing that I needed most: help.

I stepped around the back of one of the cars that was in process of restoration, and that's when I saw it. There, alone in a corner of my garage all by itself, was my motorcycle. I froze as memories of the last time I had seen it flashed through my mind: a wet mountainside in West Virginia where this nightmare had begun. The sight of that mud-splattered bike brought back all the questions from that day. "What if I had been going a little faster?" "What if I'd been going a little slower?" "Maybe if I had turned one way instead of another." It was a numbing moment as I relived that crash scene, remembering the last time I had seen my bike, lying beneath me with my legs draped across it on that cold, West Virginia mountain.

A pile of all the riding gear I'd been wearing on the day of the crash was near my bike. I say all my gear, but this isn't exactly true. My jersey and riding pants were gone. They had been cut off of me at the hospital. I slowly picked up my helmet, expecting it to be split open from one end to the other. The helmet had to have been destroyed as I recalled that indescribable, bone-crushing sound of the impact. It was shocking to see that the only visible damage was that the front visor had been torn off and there was a two or three inch scuffmark where my head had hit the rock. The hit could not have been more centered on the crown of my head. What if it hadn't been so squared on my head, maybe a little to the right, or the left? It might have been one of the many glancing blows I had experienced many times during my riding years. One of those dust yourself off and hop back on the bike moments, or a get back on the horse that threw you kind of thing. All of these futile questions didn't mean a thing now. What was done was done.

I realized with finality that I would never be able to ride again. Over 30 years of riding was over. I had loved it, and to this day, I still love it. I see guys in the spring of the year with their bikes loaded and ready to ride and I envy them.

I've never been addicted to drugs, and for me it's hard to comprehend how people who are addicted can continue doing things so harmful to their bodies. But in a way, I kind of understand the addiction thing. I was a speed junky all my life; I always wanted to go fast. There was never anything better than throwing my leg over a bike and flying. Even though the crash nearly cost me my life—certainly cost me my body—I still crave that feeling.

I'm often asked if I would ever allow our twins to ride motorcycles or four-wheelers. Shortly before the crash, we had already bought Bailey and Bryce riding jerseys and helmets in expectation that we would go bike shopping when I returned from West Virginia. I have a different perspective now. I don't want to sound hypocritical, but I wouldn't buy a bike or gear for them. When the kids get older, if they are determined to ride it will be their own decision and they can do so with their own money. My years of riding are part of who I am and I wouldn't change that, but I don't believe I could bring myself to support my kids' involvement now that I have become a statistic of the sport. I couldn't face for them, what I've had to live through.

I'm sure that I'm no different than most riders; I never even considered it possible that I could crash so badly that I wouldn't fully recover from it. In fact, this crash didn't even qualify for the top ten as far as brutality for me. Over the years I'd had much faster, harder, and uglier crashes than this one, and I did nothing more than get up and shake it off. Sure a few broken bones and stitches, minor surgery and such, but all repairable and I'd just chalked it up as a riding expense. Let's face it; every rider has the mentality that these severe isolated injuries are not going to happen to *me*.

The sobering truth is, these life-shattering injuries *are* happening to somebody. Right now those people are just statistical numbers, but by the end of each year those numbers will be names with lives attached.

Dexterity continued to be a problem, even with simple tasks such as getting dressed or showering. I was still unable to button shirts or get my shoes and socks on. Tina not only had to get herself ready in the mornings, but she had to get me ready, too. I'm not going to lie; there was an upside to my situation. Being unable to shower myself meant Tina had to crawl in with me for cleanliness therapy. As I progressed, I could eventually shower myself but I played possum for as long as I could before she caught on and made me fly solo. A sad day, indeed.

Tina normally worked three days a week at an accounting firm. But from January 1 to April 30 each year it was tax time and she worked five, sometimes six, days a week. My mom stayed on with us until mid-March to handle the housekeeping, cooking, and babysitting chores. Once a month, when she went back to Missouri, my Uncle Howard came out and took her place, efficiently keeping us all going.

Toward the end of Mom's stay is when I started driving again. It felt bizarre to get behind the wheel, something I hadn't done for the past six months. Fortunately I had always worked the gas and brake pedals with both feet; this was an advantage in my current condition with one side being more paralyzed than the other. It was liberating to know I wouldn't have to spend my life being driven around like Miss Daisy. I began timidly. After all, this was the first time in my life that I was actually afraid of speed. As my confidence grew, driving began feeling more normal and my uneasiness subsided. Another important hurdle effectively cleared.

I continued to show progress in my recovery, but walking was a thinking challenge for me. For most people, walking is a natural reflex. You walk without considering all your body does in order to move you. With the damage of paralysis, the communication lines from the brain to the muscles are short-circuited and delayed. For me, the mechanics of walking had to be broken down into segments. As I walked, I was literally thinking through each motion, a choreographed process of flex and release each muscle group required to move a leg forward. Because of this segmented walking, it was impossible to walk with a natural stride. I appeared jerky and unsteady as I gave step-by-step commands to my extremities. I'm sure I appeared to some as if I had just spent an all-nighter at the bar.

Walking continues to be my biggest challenge. This hasn't changed even after all these years and I will deal with it for the rest of my life. Because of my unsteadiness, I fall quite often. The paralysis affects my body's right side more than the left giving me the appearance of having had a stroke. My instinctive reflexes are almost non-existent, so I don't have the ability to catch myself when I fall. Like the line in the old commercial says, "I've fallen and I can't get up!" Necessity has taught me how to fall. When I know the ground's approaching, I tuck and roll like an expert. As long as it's not painful I can generally laugh it off, and I'm no longer sensitive when people (sometimes strangers) have to help me up off the ground. What's a guy to do?

People are generally kind and helpful by nature. They want to pick me up off the ground, oftentimes yanking me up so fast that I get a nosebleed. For all of you helpers out there, I got down here by myself, give me a minute and I'll get back up by myself. I wasn't hurt falling, but I might get whiplash from your helping hand.

In all seriousness, it's a testament to our fellow man of how much we want to help others. People do care about each other, contrary to the 5 o'clock news. Doors are opened for me, packages are carried, and seats are offered up—all this from total strangers, some twice my age.

For years I had been the one who offered assistance, holding doors open as a courtesy for those who needed my help. Now I am on the receiving end of that kind of thoughtfulness. I didn't perceive myself as needy in the beginning, but as I stepped back and looked at myself, I understood better what others were seeing through their eyes. One elderly gentleman, who might have been close to 90 years old and was struggling with his own motion issues, held a door open for me with a cheery, "Us guys have to stick together!" Even today I watch with envy as the senior citizens of this world stride briskly through life. I often think to myself, *I wish I could walk that well.*

Anytime I enter a room, I can feel watchful eyes judging my walk and maybe wondering what happened to me. An 80-year-old with a cane is not unusual; a 40-year-old with one raises questions. Sometimes people only give me a furtive glance, but kids aren't afraid to flat out gawk. Occasionally I'll get a question, "What'd you do to your leg?" like it was only temporary and would get better. I wish that were true. They probably think I've had a stroke, suffer from multiple sclerosis, or maybe I am just plastered, especially if I happen to get out of my car without my cane. I don't mind the questions at all and really prefer being asked to staring and wondering. You should see the startled looks when I tell people I was paralyzed from the neck down, just like the actor Christopher Reeve. The typical response is, "You've got to be kidding. Wow, you're doing pretty darn good then!" Knowing the road I've traveled, I'd have to say that's the understatement of the year.

I was still in recovery mode and seeing meaningful progress. I hadn't begun to work full time yet, but it was time that I stretched my wings to see what I could do. Since I hadn't seen a client since early October 2004, I felt out of the groove. I had been doing this job for years, but now I felt like a rookie again. How was I going to be perceived by my clients? Would new clients be able to see past my disability and trust my financial judgment? The majority of my contact with them was in their homes. I had to be able to physically get there and navigate any areas that would be problems for me. In sales, we're told to hit the pavement, but for me that could be a literal event—complete with full hospital accommodations.

One of our agents had been in a wheelchair since his teenage years. He was a quadriplegic from a level C6 (high chest) spinal cord injury, the result of a diving accident. Even though he was confined to a wheelchair for life, he made his house calls in a specially equipped van that allowed his clients to come out to his mobile office. We all respected and admired his fortitude because he made the very most from a very bad situation. I thought I understood the problems he must have faced, but until I experienced it first-hand, I realized I truly had no idea what he dealt with on a daily basis.

I started by fielding client phone calls, which generally began with a cordial "How're you doing?" or "What's new?" How do you answer what's new in 25 words or less? Well, where do I start? But these were business calls, not a time for me to unload my personal problems on them. They wanted to talk about their financial stuff, not hear a Dear Abby sob story. After all, when you ask people how they're doing you don't really expect them to say, "Well, I almost died a few months back, but thanks for asking."

My new life gained momentum. In early 2005 a fellow agent set up a client dinner presentation, and while I attended with him, I only occupied a corner chair. At that point I couldn't even visualize standing for an hour before a group of perspective clients presenting our financial program. I wondered if my future presentations would be done from a chair. In March of 2005, I was scheduled to speak at a client dinner. I was ready but worried that my legs wouldn't hold me up for that long a period of time. I made it through, on my feet, although it was exhausting, the most exhausting thing I had done since my accident. But, another milestone had been checked off.

At least for now I was back to work.

12
Patient of the Year

A few months after I had returned home, I received a letter from RHI. Expecting the usual bill, I was surprised when I opened the envelope to find a letter informing me I had been nominated for the Patient of the Year award for 2004. I had never even considered being privileged enough to see my name on that auspicious sidewalk.

My name was going to be added to God's Sidewalk surrounding RHI. A brick would tell the story of my time there, my fight, and my success. This would be a fitting honor to a glorious God who had given me the gift of a new life. Future RHI patients, maybe some like me, might wonder what we had done to deserve a brick on this path. Real names of real people who had persevered, and despite all odds, hadn't given up.

In April of 2005, along with family and friends, I attended the Patient of the Year ceremony at RHI. When I learned that the director would be sharing stories with the audience about each individual nominee's time at RHI, I wondered what my story would be. When my presentation time came, the director told a story I had related to my therapist Amy about how, for years, I had been able to ride a skateboard on my hands. Her comment, "It's a wonder you didn't end up here sooner!" got a good chuckle from the crowd.

I assumed that was my one story the director would tell, but I could feel my face flush hot when he started to relate the story of my pants falling down in the middle of the therapy gym. I thought to myself, *no, he isn't actually going there.* Guess what? Oh yes he is! The audience of over 200 howled with laughter when they turned my way and saw, standing behind me, two of the spinal injury ward nurses holding up "10" signs to score my drawer-dropping performance. Even all these years later, this anecdote and my score are still being shared with staff and patients alike.

As I looked around the attending crowd I spotted Justin, who was also a Patient of the Year nominee. I hadn't seen him for nearly four months. His metal halo had been removed and he appeared to be steadier and stronger than the last time I had seen him. He smiled at me as our eyes met, understanding what we had both been through.

Several years later, during a conversation with one of the therapists, I learned just what walking miracles Justin and I were. Since the time we had been released from RHI, nearly 30,000 patients had passed through that facility. My question to her was, "How many quadriplegic patients since Justin and I have achieved our level of recovery and walked out of here?"

"You mean with the same severity?" she asked.

"Yes."

"Zero."

My jaw dropped at her response. What are the odds of 30,000 people revolving through RHI and only two recovering to that level at basically the same time? Why us? Why were we so blessed with a recovery that was seemingly denied to so many others?

I've given those "why" questions a lot of thought over the years, and although I still don't have an answer, a friend recently gave me some food for thought.

"You know, G.L.," she said, "God loves mankind so much that He gave each one of us the gift of a free will. And we both know the crippling effects your choices have had on your life, even before the accident."

"I couldn't agree more," I told her. "I can't tell you how many times I've hit the replay button in my mind and wondered how my life might be different today had I made different choices…especially that day on the mountain."

"I know, but have you ever considered that your choices may also be the reason you're walking today instead of living a different kind of life?"

Now she had my attention. "What choices are you talking about?"

"Think about it, G.L. When you came to the point of your crisis of faith, which was when you heard God speak to your heart and tell you that everything was going to be okay, you had a choice to make. You could have chosen to believe what the medical experts said, that you were going to be a quadriplegic for the rest of your life, or you could choose to believe what God said."

I hadn't really looked at it like that before, but what she said intrigued me. "Go on," I said.

"Well, after you chose to believe God, the next thing you did was act on what you believed. You began to attack your therapy with the same 'no fear' attitude that you had ridden with all those years. And then you started telling everyone who would listen to you that you were going to walk out of RHI—despite the fact that almost no one with your level of injury had done that before."

"I remember saying over and over again to myself that I could do *anything* through Christ who strengthens me," I told her. "And while

I may not know with certainty the answers to my 'why' questions this side of Heaven, one thing I know for sure is that with God, *all things are possible.*"

When I was released from RHI in December of 2004, there was no way of knowing what my eventual functionality would be. I had already gone so much farther than anyone had ever dreamed. The RHI staff had seen cases where progress had continued for as much as two years post-trauma. As time went on, some of the heaviness that I'd felt in my arms and legs, especially on the right side, started to ease up. Instead of feeling like they weighed 100 pounds each, they felt more like 90, or even 80 pounds. Although I moved sluggishly, it was an improvement.

Even today I continue to have residual heaviness, and my whole body has the pins and needles feeling similar to what a person experiences when an arm or leg goes to sleep, though with me, the sensation is 24/7. This sensation was really annoying at first, but although it's hard to believe, now I've pretty much gotten used to it. I have the dexterity of a boxer wearing heavy boxing gloves. My fingers feel like they are the size of Polish sausages, especially on my right side, and I need to visually see an object to know that I have grasped it. My sensation of touch in the fingertips is almost non-existent.

My progress reached its plateau sometime between the second and third year after I left RHI. I assure you that I am grateful for all I have, but I'd be lying if I didn't admit that I was heartbroken when the progress stopped. I had to realize that this was most likely as good as it was going to get, and that the rest of my life was going to be a struggle. I selfishly wanted more, but how blessed I feel for all I have. You've heard people say, "It could have been worse." Well it was once *a lot worse,* and I'm reminded of that every time I visit RHI.

Every day now, I see the rest of my life as a gift, and I want to utilize that gift and share it with all who will listen. I've now lived many years longer than I might have without God's intervention. When I'm busy and the kids want my time and attention, it's so much easier now to stop what I'm doing and be Dad. When I find myself getting short-tempered with them, I am better able to step back and ask myself, is this really worth it? My mom's favorite saying, "Don't sweat the small stuff," means more now than it ever did. I try to see my life now on the wide-screen, looking at all aspects and assigning importance.

<hr />

The biggest part of my life was spent riding the church pew, attending when it was convenient for *me*, always ready with an excuse when asked, "Where have you been?" Going to church was less about building a relationship with Christ and more about going because I felt required to. What it boiled down to was this: I was afraid of going to hell. I therefore believed that if I just made it through the front door on Sundays that I was fulfilling my obligation, making sure that I had fire insurance, so to speak. I wanted to serve my tour of duty for 60-90 minutes each week then don't bother me and *maybe* I'll be back next week—providing Saturday night hasn't been too rowdy.

From time to time church members would approach me about getting involved in committee work or service projects. Up to that point, my only contribution had been to play shortstop on the church softball team. Outside of that meaningful commitment, my usual answer was, "I'm too busy." I knew church service work was important, but for someone else. That wasn't my thing.

After sitting pathetically on the sidelines for so many years, this whole life-altering event had opened my eyes and made me understand that we are a community of God. We all must be responsible to each other and for the success of the Church, which is known as the Body of Christ. The world, in general, is divided into two groups, the *givers* and the *takers*, and not necessarily split 50-50, probably more like 80-20. Individuals with an habitual taker mentality do nothing more than drain resources from society and the local church, selfishly hoarding their time and energy for themselves.

Honestly, for years I was perfectly content to be a taker, which cost me nothing in terms of time or money. But after witnessing firsthand the generosity of those who are givers, I was overwhelmed. To be on the receiving end of such self-sacrifice was humbling. Experiencing people genuinely giving of their time to visit me, call me, send cards, or bring food was a true awakening as to what it means to be a real giver. My old way of thinking, "That's fine, but let someone else take care of that," wasn't going to cut it anymore. I mean, imagine where society or the church would be if everyone thought, "Let the other guy do it." The ugly truth is, many people in the world do their best to avoid commitment, and being a giver is what commitment is all about.

Now, at times I'm over-committed because I don't want to say no when people ask for my time. This is okay, but I must remember to maintain a good balance in my life for the sake of my family. As I slowly began accepting responsibilities in our church, it was soon evident to me that the blessing of giving runs both directions. There are always going to be people out there who are in need. Sometimes they just need a smile, a kind word, or a willing ear.

People began saying to me, "I can't quite put my finger on it, but something is different about you." They were right; I felt different. Life was joyful again, life was cool, and God had left me here to live it to the fullest. The old saying, "Everything happens for a reason," may not apply to all situations, but it certainly applied to mine.

It seems that sometimes God can't make use of us until we have sunk so far down in the darkness that there is no way to go but up. I'm embarrassed to admit that I'm one of those guys who needed to be hit between the eyes with a two-by-four in order to get my attention. I sure wish I had listened to the whispers from God before the shouts came. Just at my lowest point, when I thought I was finished and done, God stepped in and said, "Oh no, not only are you not done, I'm just getting started with you."

After almost a decade of church membership (the first half of that time, membership would have been a very loose term), the unexpected happened; I was asked to step into a leadership role of serving as a deacon. This floored me because five years earlier this opportunity would have been totally incomprehensible. I quickly told my minister, Burt, and the church elders that I wasn't ready yet for this responsibility. I already had a couple of perceptions of what a deacon was to be. First and foremost, a deacon leads by example, and I felt comfortable with that. It was my second perception that terrified me. I truly thought I had to have all the biblical answers to any question the membership might pose to me. I soon realized that not only did I *not* have all the answers, but that I would *never* have all the answers. In fact I don't believe that on this earth we will ever fully achieve spiritual perfection, and I think that's by design.

I don't think God ever intended for His people to have *all* the answers. That's where faith and trust come in. Everyone knows someone who arrogantly believes that God has blessed them with all the answers of the universe. If you don't mind me saying, give me a break! If God's vastness is as big as an ocean and our brain is the size of a soup can, what makes *anyone* think they could totally understand God with the small amount we are able to scoop into it? By reading the Bible, studying with fellow Christians, and walking together in our Christian ideals, we strengthen each other. Proverbs 27:17 says, *As iron sharpens iron, so one man sharpens another.*

***

In the fall of 2006 I was invited to participate in an event called the Walk to Emmaus, a Christian men's retreat. Not being familiar with the weekend program, my first thought was *maybe this isn't for me because I sure can't walk very far.* I was reminded that the title was derived from the biblical story of Jesus walking with two strangers on their way to the town of Emmaus following His resurrection. Jesus wasn't recognized on this walk until they had arrived in Emmaus, and then their eyes were opened to Christ's presence. So as with that first walk to Emmaus, this program was intended to open our eyes and build strong Christian leadership.

You can participate in the walk as a pilgrim only once in your life. After that, you are welcome and encouraged to attend as a volunteer worker. I felt mentally and physically ready for the Emmaus experience, but I definitely got more than I anticipated. What a powerful weekend. I came away knowing positively that I was ready to commit myself even deeper to God's plan for me.

I returned home with a clearer direction from God for my life. I knew that I wanted to step more fully into a leadership role in my church, serving in whatever capacity I could. No more sitting on the sidelines; it was time to take to the field. I accepted the nomination to serve as deacon. My first year's service would be on a trial basis, which allowed either the church or me to decide if this step was right for both. This would be followed by an additional three-year commitment if we agreed to proceed. During that first year I became more committed to both Christ and to my church, eagerly seeking to learn more. And in 2011 I was nominated to become an elder.

I developed an at-home Bible study group for families, which I greatly enjoyed, but my most challenging role was that of a rotating Sunday school teacher for our children's class, ages 5-12 years. It was both impressive and terrifying at the same time, once I discovered how much these kids knew. A few of the students ranked right up there with some of the adults when it came to knowledge of the Bible. I worried that the day would come when some five-year-old would stump me with a Bible question. How embarrassing would that be?

One Sunday, on the way to church, my daughter, Bailey, and I were discussing that day's upcoming lesson. I told her, "I hear we have some new faces in class." She rolled her eyes as she answered, "Yeah, good luck today Dad, you're gonna need it." She was right; it was a class full of lively kids who behaved as if they were all on a sugar high. I survived the day, but just barely.

On the way home after church that day, I commented to her, "You weren't kidding Bailey. Some of those kids don't listen too well. And you know how Dad does with kids who don't listen."

She laughed, "Yeah Dad, I can't believe you didn't have a melt down today."

13
Perspective Is Everything

I work hard to maintain a normal life. However, some roles have by necessity been reversed between Tina and I. The natural order of the way things get done around our house is different than it used to be. Tina must provide the physical strength for some of our home maintenance projects, while I've learned to handle more domestic jobs. The kids claim Dad makes the best Hamburger Helper *ever*, which is a real improvement over my pre-crash Pop Tart casseroles.

I try my best to downplay my limitations by making light of my struggle. When I do fall, as long as there isn't blood involved, I can generally laugh it off. I always used to joke and say I should have been the poster child for the *No Fear* bumper sticker—now I feel like the poster child for the old commercial where the woman says, "I've fallen and I can't get up!"

Sometimes it's not so easy to laugh it off. Recently, when I tripped in the garage, I dropped a metal shearer which impaled my right hand all the way through. Since this is a family-oriented book I'll only admit to saying *ouch!* This mishap occurred in April, making my church friends question, "Did you do that in honor of Easter?"

Mishaps are a normal part of my life now since I quite often struggle to accomplish what should be simple tasks. I was never much of a winter person before, but now I downright hate the season. I had no idea what cold could do to an already stressed out nervous system. A bad situation becomes worse with cold and damp weather. My muscles stiffen and at times even lock up to the point where moving is almost impossible. A normal person might feel a slight chill, but I have experienced episodes of uncontrollable shivering that resemble convulsions. I could happily live the rest of my life in an 80-degree environment, toasty and happy.

Recently, I was returning from a client's home that was over an hour away from my house. It was a frigid Friday night around 9:30 when I thought the car seemed to be steering funny. When I pulled over to look, to my horror I immediately saw the problem: my worst nightmare—a flat tire. The temperature had fallen to -2° and here I was in a suit and tie. What was I going to do? This wasn't just cold; this was dangerous cold. I barely have the strength and dexterity to change a tire in warm weather, there was *no way* it was going to happen in this extreme cold. If my muscles locked up under these conditions while I was outside the car, I could literally freeze to death. Pre-crash this never would have been an issue; now it could be life or death.

I had no choice but to drive on the flat tire to a nearby auto parts store. Nothing else was open. Fortunately for me, there were two guys shopping in the store who were willing to change my tire. I felt so bad. Not only was it difficult for me to ask for help for what any man would consider a simple task, but to top it off, the two weren't dressed for spending any extended time outside in this cold weather. Those poor guys didn't even have gloves, yet they were willing to help me out. It was a pride-swallowing experience. I desperately needed them, and guys, if you're reading this book, God bless you!

When you start off your early life with a broken back, there is nowhere to go but downhill. This may not mean much to those fortunate ones who have never had to deal with back problems. My issues began with my first major crash when I was 18 years old. Even after years of weight lifting and strength conditioning, it still was just a matter of time before I would start experiencing real problems. Bulging and herniated disks became the norm. Now, because of my paralysis leaving me with such an abnormal stride, walking has done nothing but compound my already vulnerable back situation.

Since my crash, my back has deteriorated to the point of requiring spinal injections almost yearly. The injections only buy me time from any future surgery. The very real concern is that my current paralysis would seriously limit rehabilitation following such surgery. The last thing I want is to have surgery and end up back in a wheelchair for good. I've been down that road once already; I don't have any plans of regressing.

When I was at RHI, I had every intention of returning to work for good, even when I was encouraged to apply for Social Security disability. By the time I'd finished rehab and returned home, things were different. My back problems, my instability, and my susceptibility to cold temperatures helped make the decision to exercise the disability provision in my Ozark pension plan. This wasn't exactly the early retirement I had planned, but it seemed like a logical course and I felt truly blessed to have this option available to me.

I also applied for Social Security disability, expecting the usual reams of paperwork and endless delays. Social Security required that I be certified by one of its own doctors. The good thing with paralysis (if there is a good thing) is, you either have it or you don't, making for an easy diagnosis as well as impossible to fake. I was approved immediately, and in 2009 began drawing my retirement and disability benefits.

Over the years, figuring out my limitations has been a learning process. Even though I've tried to maintain a normal life, some lessons have been learned the hard way. I forget sometimes that my physical abilities can hinder me because my mind still remembers a fully functioning body. At times, the brain fails to recognize that it is dragging along a sluggish, uncooperative mass. The communication lines are spotty and sometimes short-circuited. Like a cell phone with only one bar, my brain asks my body, "Can you hear me now?"

No lesson was learned at greater risk than when we were vacationing with friends, Dale & Nancy Depping, at their lake home on Lake of the Ozarks, Missouri, in July of 2009. Since the crash, we had spent every Fourth of July there enjoying the lake, boating, swimming, and spending time with these dear friends. The lake itself presented obstacles. Someone always has to help me down to and back from the dock, like an invalid old man.

On this particular day, we took the boat out on the lake. I've learned that boating satisfies my need for speed. While someone else drives, I just hang on and grin. As we neared the cove where their lake house was, we cut the motor. I had always been a good swimmer, and even post-crash I had learned to tread water efficiently. Although the water in the cove was rough, I decided to take a routine dip in the lake, not knowing that the situation was about to turn deadly.

When the wind suddenly picked up, it not only caused the water to become rougher, but to my horror the boat began to drift away faster than I was able to swim to catch it. I was in trouble. In a matter of seconds, not only was I unable to catch the boat, they were too far away to even throw me a lifeline. Fatigue set in rapidly in my limbs as I struggled to stay afloat. The driver of the boat, Dennis, was desperately trying to turn back toward me but things were happening too quickly. I was already taking in mouthfuls of water as the waves were washing over me.

I was starting to panic big time; I didn't know how much longer

I could stay up. Not knowing the gravity of the situation, our host Nancy, approached me on her jet ski. She casually yelled out, "Are you okay G.L.?"

I quickly responded in a panicky voice, "No, I need a life jacket *now!*"

Nancy understood there was a problem, but maybe not the serious extent of it. I was going down if something wasn't done immediately. Nancy's granddaughter was riding with her, and the girl was frantically trying to get her life jacket off so she could throw it to me. Nancy made several passes around me, trying to get close enough for me to grab onto the Jet Ski while her granddaughter continued struggling with the buckles on her life jacket. By the fourth pass around me, I knew I either had to grab onto the Jet Ski or get hold of a life jacket. There wasn't going to be time for another pass; I was going down. I yelled to Nancy as best I could while gulping water, "Throw me *your* life jacket—*now!*"

All options were gone; it had to be now. I prayed that Nancy could hit the mark with her jacket. If she missed me, there wouldn't be time for another go around. This was about as all or nothing as you could get, and with my panic came a clear sense of déjà vu. Just as with my 2004 crash, I was on a harmless routine weekend get-away that could cost me my life. Before I went down again, Nancy hit me dead in the face with her life jacket and I wanted to scream "Yeah, baby!"

How can I describe the feeling of having cheated death a second time? It's not that I'm afraid to die—even though most of my life I couldn't have said that—but I want to raise my kids, grow old with my wife, and finish the job God intends for me.

We all learned some valuable lessons that day. First, G.L. is not a good swimmer. Second, G.L. is not a good swimmer. Third, and most important, G.L. doesn't go near the lake again without his water wings on. In all seriousness, I was reminded again on that day that *life is fragile* and to quit taking chances with it. I think about the "what ifs" of life more seriously now without becoming a worrywart. One thing is for sure: Nancy Depping saved my life that day.

Life gives us opportunities to experience many types of lessons. One summer day I was driving alone back to Missouri to take my father-in-law a 1956 Mercury that he had purchased. Even though I assumed it would be the normal road trip, just for added insurance, I loaded up my toolbox for the "just in case." You never know with a 50+-year-old car what might come up.

Half way through the trip, I realized the one item I should have brought was a gas can. As that old nag sputtered and spit, I thought to myself, *oh no, it can't be!* The gas gauge was still showing over a quarter of a tank, but unbeknownst to me, the gauge didn't work. I drifted onto the shoulder of the interstate and let the car roll to a stop. Since I had just passed an exit a couple of miles back, I wasn't concerned. After all, a classic car and a cripple guy with a cane, I surely looked harmless enough. I'll just stick my thumb out and wait for a ride, right? Wrong!

It wasn't long before I got the message that no one was going to stop. Again, since this is a family book, I just said *shoot!* I started walking along the shoulder of the highway back toward that exit I had just passed, cane in hand and traffic blazing by me. I was already unstable on my feet, so each time a semi-truck whooshed by me at 70 mph its draft would almost blow me over. I truly feared for my life, at times hanging onto the guardrail as the truckers flew by. It actually crossed my mind that after all I had been through, this surely wasn't going to be the way I was going to die, squished like road kill! I must have looked pretty pitiful, because by the time I arrived at the gas station, the attendant felt so sorry for me that he offered to take me and the gas can back to the car himself. A valuable lesson was learned that day: don't leave home without a gas can.

Surprises come in two varieties, good and bad. One late spring after I had completed my pilgrim walk for Emmaus, the alumni participants held a fellowship dinner. I was surprised when, for the first time, I was asked to publically share my story. I was a comfortable public speaker because, after all, it had been part of my job for the past 21 years. However, this speech wasn't about financial planning, which placed me a little out of my comfort zone. This would be the story of both my darkest and brightest hours, lumped together in one package. It was an emotional presentation for them and for me. We all cried. I had never told my story all the way through before, and many places were tough for me to relive, especially with Tina being there.

A Baptist minister happened to be part of the audience that night, and afterward he invited me to come to his church to share my story with the congregation. I agreed, not really understanding until closer to the time that he intended my talk to take the place of his Sunday sermon. Only the second time in my life I was to share my story to a small crowd, and I was to be the preacher for the day.

The closer that Sunday got, the more nervous I became. I didn't want to stand in the pulpit; I wasn't qualified for that. I wasn't a preacher, just barely a teacher; I was just a walking miracle with a story to tell. But I had a strong desire to touch lives and make people understand that God does still perform miracles and is willing to forgive, even when we don't deserve it. It wasn't easy, but I made it through that presentation.

Following the service, many members of the congregation approached me saying things like, "Oh, I wish my brother (or my neighbor or my parent) could have been here today. They're struggling (either physically or spiritually) and I believe their being here would have greatly impacted them." I wasn't expecting these kinds of statements and I was surprised. In the years that have passed since that time, I've received the same comments nearly 100 percent of the time when I speak. It didn't take me long to figure out why this scenario kept playing itself out. The sobering truth is, everyone knows someone who is hurting and is in need of encouragement.

Now the wheels were starting to turn, slowly at first, but gathering momentum. God was carefully preparing me to be used for His purpose, but in a way that wouldn't overwhelm me in the beginning.

I was excited to be able to volunteer as a worker at the next Emmaus Walk. After all, my own pilgrim walk had been a powerful experience and I was anxious to share my story with the new pilgrims. The center point of the weekend was always the powerful personal testimonies that were weaved into the fabric of gospel lessons. As a rookie team member, I expected that I would be assigned to kitchen duty or clean-up detail, the behind the scenes things that keep the program running smoothly.

The volunteer team has numerous preparation meetings leading up to the weekend walk. Before the meetings even started, I received in the mail an outline format of one of the planned talks. The outline didn't say who the speaker was; I just hoped it would be someone good. I assumed this was a talk we would hear at the first prep meeting, allowing the team to preview its content. Unfortunately, a scheduling conflict kept me from attending that first meeting. Knowing I wouldn't get to hear the speaker's preview talk, I pitched the format in the trash and went on about my business.

At the next meeting, my face turned red when the director of the walk asked me if my talk was ready. He said that since I'd missed the previous meeting, I was now scheduled to preview my talk at an upcoming meeting. I couldn't believe what I was hearing and I'm sure I stood there with my mouth hanging open.

No one had called me, no one had told me *I* was to be on the schedule. I told the director that I couldn't possibly be giving a talk. This was my first time on the volunteer team and besides, I'd already thrown the outline in the trash.

"There must be a mistake," I said.

The director quickly and loudly responded, "You threw the outline in the *trash*?"

Since then, we have become very good friends, but at that time I'm sure he was probably thinking, "What a doofus!"

I managed to redeem myself and the preview talk went smoothly. Since that time, I continue to volunteer and share my testimony at the walk. I am often asked, "Isn't it hard to relive that day again?" It's odd in a way. While being able to share my story is therapeutic to some degree, parts of it still bring out raw emotions, not that it's a bad thing. My honest emotions are deeply shared by my audience, allowing them to travel down that desperate road with me.

In the world today, people resist exposing themselves to any kind of vulnerability for fear of appearing weak, but when faced with real raw emotion, it tends to break down that barrier and thus opens their hearts. Let's face it, God best reaches an open heart. The Emmaus team laughingly refers to my talk as the "Kleenex talk" because by the time I finish we are all usually crying. I've always asked for God's guidance, saying, "What is it you want me to do?" I didn't know at that point where God was leading me.

I certainly credit the Walk to Emmaus program for helping to begin my speaking career. From the very beginning, team members and ministers volunteering with the walk would ask me to share my story with their churches. Doors were being opened for me to share my message at a rapid pace. As I was approached more and more often, I struggled to comprehend where all this was going.

I remember lying in that hospital in Huntington, West Virginia, totally paralyzed, questioning then whether this was the life God had in mind for me. During the years following my crash, His plan was beginning to be revealed. I'm still blown away by how God can take our darkest hour and turn it into something to glorify His power.

"For I know the plans I have for you," declares the LORD, "plans to prosper you and not to harm you, plans to give you hope and a future (Jeremiah 29:11).

14
Let's Learn Together

I had been searching for a new doctor closer to home, one with the expertise capable of dealing with my paralysis. At the Emmaus Walks, it's preferred that you check your job at the door in order to avoid being distracted. Career choices aren't discussed, which is why you never hear, "So, what do you do for a living?"

After my first talk at the Emmaus Walk, a man by the name of Earl Craig approached me, asking me about my paralysis and injury. I was used to being questioned, but I could tell during the course of our conversation that Earl must have some medical background because his questions weren't run of the mill. They were more technical and involved. He asked who my doctor was and I told him. But I also conveyed to him that I was interested in finding someone closer to home.

His next comment caught me off guard, "Why don't you come and see me? This happens to be my field of expertise." Not only had I now found a doctor, but a Christian doctor with the experience I needed. It was a good fit. We now have more than just a professional relationship; Earl and I are good friends.

I didn't realize then that God was building another piece of the framework for my story, a new avenue that I had never considered. Up to this point I had been speaking solely to churches and faith-based organizations. Now, Earl approached me about joining him at the Indiana University School of Medicine. Earl, Dr. Craig, was responsible for presenting an annual spinal cord lecture to first year medical students. The main thrust of his lecture for these future doctors was how to determine where a patient has injured their spinal cord and the prognosis for life expectancy based on the motor skills they have lost. He thought it would be beneficial for students to hear from someone who had experienced the kind of injury they were learning about.

Students are taught that paraplegics (those who have lost all motor skills from the waist down) have usually sustained cord damage near the T1 to L2 level of the spinal column. Naturally, as the injury site rises up the spinal column, the loss of functioning skills is greater. At the C6 level (approximately high-chest), students are taught that it's possible for the patient to eventually graduate to a regular wheelchair that they can operate on their own, rolling the wheels with their own hands. But at the C5 level (low neck), a patient is most likely expected to use a motorized wheelchair with a joystick. The chart goes no higher than C5 because at that level the patient has lost every motor skill.

During this annual lecture, these future doctors hear for the first time the phrase "C5 keeps you alive." The reason they say that C5 keeps you alive is because at C4 the outcome of the injury gets deadly serious. At C4, not only is there a total loss of motor skills, but the injury also becomes life threatening. Once paralysis sets in on the diaphragm, the victim loses the ability to breathe. As most people remember with actor Christopher Reeve, following his accident he spent the rest of his life with a ventilator in his neck.

Then comes the big one, C3. Basically, students are taught not to expect to see many C3 or above injuries because the majority of those victims die at the scene of the accident. They suffocate.

Everyone has heard people say that God doesn't perform miracles anymore. What people and doctors sometimes fail to recognize is that God performs miracles each and every day in this world. I sustained a C3 injury and, by all accounts from the medical community, I should've never made it off that mountain alive on that cold October day in 2004. My survival has been the miracle of my life, a gift from God.

My purpose in being with Dr. Craig at IU is to help the students understand that the textbook prognosis is not always the reality. I share the experience of the crash, giving specific details of how I was paralyzed. Normally patients with this kind of injury are rendered unconscious, but I remained fully alert and aware throughout the whole ordeal.

The students always want to know things from me that they can't find in a textbook. What did it feel like? How instantaneous was it or was there a bodily delay? Did it hurt? What pain did you experience? Can you feel hot and cold? All of these questions are important for them to understand, but I believe the reason I am at IU is to answer the one question that continues to be asked year after year. Without fail, students always want to know, "What got you through it?"

My answer is always this: "My doctors weren't able to do all that much for me and I don't fault them for that. I understand that their hands were tied, but when the medical community said, 'I'm sorry but there's nothing more we can do for you,' my Lord and Savior took over and said, 'Watch this!'"

Some students may never have to deal with my kind of injury, but down the road, unfortunately, others will. And when they do, I hope they will remember that back in medical school they once met a walking C3 spinal cord injury patient, and they will say, "Overcoming this injury can be possible. Maybe not through our works, but it *can* be possible." My prayer is that more lives will be affected in a positive way by doctors who are willing to hold on to hope just a little longer, instead of giving up.

In the years that I've been speaking at Indiana University, I've come to the place where I can almost always anticipate the questions that will arise—until recently, that is. This year, as I was fielding questions from these inquisitive medical students, one young woman was eagerly waiving her arm to be seen and have her questions answered. The first part of her questions started out innocently enough, "How has your paralysis affected your bladder and bowel movements?"

I answered her question quickly and accurately, hoping to move on to less personal issues. Then came the stunner: "How has it affected you sexually?" That question was a showstopper. A few students giggled and I couldn't help but laugh as I looked back at Earl. He was about to fall out of his chair. What first popped out of my mouth was, "I'm not sure because I've been married for 25 years and my wife won't let me touch her anymore!" The room thundered with laughter.

Not all of my speaking engagements are filled with laughter. Sometimes people will come and wish me well at the end of a speaking event, relating stories of their own life experiences, some of which are really tragic, heartbreaking stories. And in all of this, I continue to be amazed at the resiliency of the human spirit. Why is it that some people who suffer hardship grow in strength and courage while others become bitter and resentful, developing a "why me" attitude? It is sometimes hard to embrace the scripture that says *Consider it pure joy, my brothers, whenever you face trials of many kinds, because you know that the testing of your faith develops perseverance. Perseverance must finish its work so you may be mature and complete, not lacking anything* (James 1:2-3 NIV).

So are we to be happy when we struggle? Life isn't always a bed of roses and yet, ironically, I've had members of my own congregation approach me saying they have never experienced hardship in their lives. I pray for them, because it is coming. It's not a matter of *if*, but *when*. I believe with all my heart that you cannot have a real testimony until your spirit has been tested. What do you learn if your life doesn't have potholes? If we never have problems, how would we ever know that God can solve them? Being on top of the mountain looking down usually breeds arrogance and stifles growth. Nothing grows on a mountaintop; all growth occurs down in the valleys.

Not only were people sharing with me stories of their own triumphs, they were motivating me to do more. I started hearing, "You should write a book." Honestly, the first time it was mentioned I nearly laughed out loud. I mean, talk about ironic, me write a book? I hate to read. But the more I thought about it, the more I felt led to do it.

Knowing this kind of an endeavor was way beyond my capabilities, I went directly to my mother. When I was growing up, she penned a few articles for various magazines and is a voracious reader herself. Besides that, she can type. Nothing I inherited. Mom hadn't written any articles for years, but she still had the gift of being able to put my thoughts into a readable format. I didn't ask, but she immediately volunteered to help put the book together. Even though she had her own life to live and we were separated by a six-hour drive, we decided to tackle the project.

My initial thought was that we would knock this book thing out in no time and have it available quickly for upcoming speaking engagements. Well, welcome to the real world. It didn't take me long to figure out what a huge undertaking this was and truly how far in over my head I was. Writing a manuscript proved to be the hardest thing I have ever done. Well, almost.

Mom and I could only work together when her schedule would allow her to come to stay for a week at a time. I tried to work on the manuscript alone between her visits, but I never was a fast typist. With the injury, I was down to a quasi-operational left hand, and I'm not left handed. Can you imagine a hunt-and-peck manuscript getting quickly to the publisher? My original intention was not to pursue any future speaking engagements until the book was in print. It didn't take me long to realize that I might be dead before the hunt-and-peck got to press. Even with Mom's help, it was a time-absorbing process, much more than I expected. I couldn't put off the speaking requests for several years while we tried to complete the book.

As it turned out, God connected me with several experienced professionals who assisted me in transforming my manuscript into the book you now hold in your hands. Another one of His amazing miracles.

By now the phone was ringing more and more as word spread about my story. One booking would lead to three others. Because my talk is faith-based I speak mostly to churches, but occasionally I am asked to address audiences in schools or paramedic conferences or prisons. I won't turn down any opportunity because I believe God will lead me to where He wants His message heard.

Some of the churches recorded my talk, which allowed their members to have a CD of the message to take for a friend or family member who wasn't able to attend. These discs weren't mass-produced, just taken from a master copy as requested. Before long, churches were airing my message on Christian radio programs. My twins thought I was a rock star. In their eyes I may as well have been Justin Bieber or Taylor Swift.

When I first began preparing for speaking engagements, my daughter, Bailey, at that time age nine, wanted to be supportive but wasn't sure how. One day she came into my office and asked, "What are you doing, Daddy?"

"Well Sweetheart, I'm just putting some thoughts together for my talk tomorrow," I told her.

She immediately gave me a gigantic hug around the neck and uttered these prophetic words: "Daddy I sure hope you get it right tomorrow."

I laughed, but she was completely serious as she continued with her words of wisdom. "Daddy, if you forget what you're going to say tomorrow, just tell them you like candy."

I'm not sure what that meant, but it apparently made sense to a 9-year-old. At least she was honest; I do like candy. I wrote that message from her on a Post-it note, and to this day I carry it with me—just in case I forget what I'm going to say.

One of the churches where I spoke produced a DVD and they allowed me to make copies of it. Although it wasn't professional quality, I could finally make my message available to anyone who asked. This process helped me understand that I really needed professional help in developing a high quality DVD. How was this going to happen? Then came the answer in the form of yet another miracle from God.

One day in 2010, I got a call from my boss, Charlie Sharpe. Besides the fact that Charlie founded Ozark National, the company I have worked for since I was 21 years old, he is also a pastor who developed a Christian ministry called Heartland. Located on a 20,000 acre farm in northeastern Missouri, Heartland is structured to provide direction and counseling for troubled youth and adults who suffer from drug and alcohol abuse. Their success comes through an introduction of God's love, strength, and forgiveness. During this call, Charlie invited me to come to Heartland to share my story with his congregation.

Now I was excited on two fronts. First, I was thrilled to have the opportunity to share my message with such a large group and, second, I knew that all of these services were televised throughout portions of Missouri, Illinois, and Iowa. This meant I would have a professionally edited and produced DVD copy of my testimony produced on Heartland's studio quality equipment.

Here I was, worrying about how I would get a high quality DVD cut, but God already had it covered. Isn't He amazing? I decided to title the DVD *Faith 911* as the result of a dream I had one night. The numbers *911* were the racing plate numbers on my motorcycle, while true *Faith* followed the crash. Heartland's graphic department handled the entire cover design, and the studio facility produced the DVD. It was a win-win situation for me; my prayers were answered. I would now be able to offer a studio cut DVD for people to take home.

It's humbling when people say they saw me on TV or heard me on the radio. I haven't changed; I'm still just me. When God spoke to my heart to share my testimony, it certainly wasn't for any notoriety. Besides, who could have foreseen God's plan for me that day as I was lying on that cold, damp West Virginia mountain fighting for my life?

The year 2010 was my Super Bowl of life. Our church was planning a Special Needs Awareness Sunday to promote greater understanding of those with physical or mental challenges. I was asked if I would be the main speaker during the morning service. National inspirational speaker David Ring, who is known for his "I have cerebral palsy... what's your problem?" message, was to be the main speaker in the evening. I laughed as I wondered which part was assigned to me, physical or mental.

I had previously talked to a portion of our congregation during an annual Mother's Day banquet a few years earlier, but this event was my opportunity to speak to our entire membership. Mom, Dad, and my Uncle Howard came in from Missouri for the event, which happened to be on my mother's 28th anniversary of her 39th birthday (I promised I wouldn't say how old she is).

It was a wonderful service. As I shared my story, I hoped that God would use it to especially touch anyone who might be there with the same attitude that I'd once had: *I'm just here doing my religious duty, so don't bother me.* Judging from the tears and sobbing that I saw and heard from the pulpit, God was having a busy day.

When I finished my message, I took a seat down front and our minister, Burt Brock, stepped up to the pulpit and asked those who wanted to be baptized to come forward. Tina and I had been talking with the twins for quite some time about baptism, but we wanted it to be their free-will decision without any pressure. On that Sunday we didn't know if one of them, both of them, or neither of them would come forward for baptism.

Bryce immediately worked his way down the aisle. However, Bailey wasn't coming. Just when I had decided only one of them was coming forward that morning, Bailey came scurrying down the aisle, too. I closed my eyes and just thanked God.

We had previously talked about me baptizing the twins when the day arrived. Well, here it was. While Bailey and Bryce went to change into their baptismal robes, I joined our minister, Burt, as we changed into our own attire. Burt stepped into the baptismal first to steady me as I followed him. And in a moment, the twins joined us for what was to be one of the most meaningful and precious moments of our family's life.

How can any dad put into words the feeling of being the one to baptize his own children into Christ? It just doesn't get any better than this. As I looked around the sanctuary, there was hardly a dry eye in the house. What a day!

I've learned that life sometimes takes bizarre twists and turns. Lee Eckart, an elder of our church and a very good friend, was one of the three men who came faithfully to RHI to bring me communion on Sundays. When I came home from RHI, Lee was the friend I called on most frequently when I needed a helping hand.

Since our home is in the center of a five-acre lot surrounded by trees, we often relied on Lee's expertise whenever we had a questionable tree removal. Lee was a world-class, professional woodsman who was able to drop a tree exactly where he expected it to land. In fact, not only was logging his career, he also competed in professional logger competitions around the world. In his most recent achievement at that time, Lee had placed sixth in the world finals held in Sweden.

You'd be hard pressed to find a more experienced woodsman than Lee. So when, in 2011, Tina and I received a phone call telling us that Lee had sustained a critical work-related injury, we couldn't have been more stunned. Our church elders were being asked to come immediately to the hospital; the expectation was that Lee would not survive.

We found out that he had been cutting trees alone on a military base when a falling tree struck him. How the injury occurred wasn't clear, but the outcome was evident. It was nearly two hours before he was discovered unconscious, but miraculously alive. The entire mask area of Lee's face had been crushed, his skull was cracked from front to back, and bone fragments had been forced into the brain. He had been frantically loaded onto a life support helicopter and taken to Methodist Hospital, the very place where I had been flown following my accident in 2004. Not only was Lee at the same hospital, but he was also on the exact floor and only two doors down from the room I had occupied in the neurological ICU ward. Mercifully, he was in a coma and unaware of what had happened.

When I arrived at Methodist Hospital to offer my support to his family, I wasn't expecting to be overwhelmed by my own emotions and memories. The moment I arrived, I found myself re-living the same feeling of desperation that I'd experienced there seven years earlier. When I entered Lee's room I couldn't even recognize my friend; his face had been so destroyed. Lee was battling for his life, and I was in the midst of my own battle as I fought back the powerful flood of feelings that had been released.

Lee's situation was touch-and-go that night as we stayed with the family and prayed. By the next day he had rallied enough that the doctors felt that he was going to make it, but the concern was that he might fall into a vegetative state. He remained in a coma for about a week, but once he regained consciousness his improvement was steady.

After weeks of ICU and reconstructive surgery, Lee was transferred to, of all places, RHI—my alma mater. The irony of all this is still mind boggling to me. Now Lee would be fighting his way back from the edge of death and I would be the one giving all the support I knew how to give.

During a visit toward the end of his stay at RHI, I asked Lee if seven years earlier he could have ever imagined that today, in 2011, we would be reversing roles and I would be the one coming to visit him at RHI. He answered quickly, as if he had already been thinking about that very thing. He said, "You know G.L., I've heard you share your story a number of times over the years and even though it's extremely powerful, I still came away telling myself that something like that could never happen to me."

I wasn't really surprised by his response because I have no doubt that most people anticipate tragedy to happen to the other guy, just like I did. Lee also talked to me about that day in the woods when he drifted in and out of consciousness after the crushing blow to his face. He remembered briefly waking up and trying to lift his head a few inches off the ground. As he laid his head back down to the ground, he recalled the sound his broken face made...it sounded like dropping a bag of crushed ice.

Lee couldn't have been in a better facility than RHI because I believe (correction: I *know*) that miracles happen in that building. Even Lee's doctors agreed that the only explanation for his survival was that he had experienced a miracle. From a purely medical standpoint, he should have died that day out in those woods.

Sometime during his stay, Lee shared his story with one of his staff nurses. In the course of their conversation, he asked her how long she had been working at RHI, and she said she'd been there for 12 years. Then he asked her if she remembered a previous patient, a friend of his named G.L. Woods. She immediately grinned and then responded, "Did you ever hear the story about his pants falling down in the middle of the therapy gym?" It was a woman named Marijean, one of my main staff nurses whom I still visit when I go back to RHI. It seems that Marijean is doing her very best to single-handedly keep the legend of the pants alive. Surely, with passing time, it will be nothing more than folklore.

Following Lee's release from RHI and a number of months of recovery, he returned to work. To welcome him back after his long absence, his crew presented him with the limb that smacked him full-face. When he asked how they knew which limb it was, they showed him his two front teeth that were still imbedded in the limb.

Like me, my friend Lee survived a horrific accident that could very well have taken his life. For both of us, these incidents were life changing. However, unlike me, Lee was already a man of faith before his accident. Those who know him will say that his relationship with not only Christ, but with his wife and children as well, is even deeper, richer, and fuller that it was before.

I believe that Lee Eckart and I now share the same perspective about what is truly important in life.

15
A Temporary Inconvenience

Imagine your brain sending a detailed letter of instruction to your body, but by the time the letter arrives at its destination, it's only a bare bones text message containing scarcely enough information to accomplish the command. This is a perfect description of my situation. A permanent short-circuit exists in my spinal cord that alters every message that my brain sends to my body. My brain is speaking loud and clear, but my body has lost its hearing aid. This is irreparable damage that I live with daily.

I recently had a meaningful conversation with a dear friend who was aware of my active lifestyle before the crash. Knowing that I had worked out daily, was a scuba diver, a black belt, and played on the church softball team, she asked, "How do you handle going from that type of life to the one you have now?"

My answer to her was, "Because this is only a temporary inconvenience; it isn't going to last forever."

Oh, I'm not in denial. I've accepted the fact that I will probably live out my life like this, but it's still only temporary. I *will* run again someday, my God promises me that. When we get to heaven, and you see a guy running down the streets of gold like Forrest Gump ran down the back roads of Greenbow, Alabama, that'll be me.

Let's face it, people struggle with everything you can think of in this world. Hopefully, during those times they can remind themselves that whatever they are dealing with is only a temporary inconvenience. I've learned that life doesn't have to be perfect to be wonderful.

When I left RHI, the three things I wanted most were to serve my God as He desired, to be the husband that my wife deserved, and to be the father that my children so desperately needed. I believe with all my heart that there will be a day when I will be held accountable for my children's souls. I believe that it is so important for me to leave them an inheritance. Not the inheritance of homes, cars, or money, but an inheritance of the knowledge of eternity. Because, unlike material things that don't last, the knowledge of eternity will stay with them *forever.* I want to show my kids what it means to give God your best. It's sad when I look back at how many years I wasted, not only not giving God my best, but barely giving Him my second or third best.

I also want to show my kids how to find true happiness. Unfortunately, the world seems to think happiness is found in immorality, addiction, or material things. My kids need to know that happiness usually boils down to this one basic thing: if you have peace in your life, you have a pretty good chance of being happy.

Contrary to popular sentiments, merely believing in God will not bring you peace. The Bible says, *You believe that there is one God. Good! Even the demons believe that—and shudder* (James 2:19 NIV). True peace comes from trusting God. Peace comes when you can say to yourself, "I trust that what God has planned for me is the right thing." And let's face it; it's not hard to think this way when things are going smooth. However, try feeling that same way when you've just lost a loved one, just lost your job, or, like me, you've just lost your health. During those times it's okay to say to yourself, "I'm not having a good time here and this isn't fun, but I *trust* that God is right here with me, doing the right thing, at the right time, and most importantly to the right person." When you can say that, you will tap into the peace of God, which ultimately will lead to your happiness.

The sad truth is, there are millions of self-proclaimed Christians in this world who will spend a lifetime learning and reading about God's truths, and yet they will never experience any of them because they are just going through the motions. That's exactly what I did. If God's Word is not transforming the way we think, the way we talk, the way we act, the way we love, and the way we hand out compassion, then let's face it: the Bible is nothing more than a history lesson.

God didn't mean for His Word to be merely a history lesson. I believe it is important to say thank you to God, but I say be careful, because sometimes the verbal thank you can just be lip service. I've learned that the way we show God true thanks is by our actions. Just saying thank you is easy, but showing thank you actually takes effort. It took the very seriousness of my crash for me to come to understand this.

None of us know what future regrets we may be able to correct today. If you could visualize yourself 20 years down the road and think about what you would miss the most about today, it may change your perspective on what is really important in your life—now as well as in the future. I can visualize things that, 20 years ago, I thought I had to have or do, but they mean absolutely zero to me today.

When I think of all the milestones and long-lasting memories of my life, none of them contain material things. Those milestones and memories all involve meaningful relationships, love, great friends, and laughter. The lie that says he who dies with the most toys wins has been exposed. The toys don't count. Unfortunately, I paid a huge price before I finally understand what's truly important in life. But as I see it, the accident may have cost me *my body*, but it saved *my eternal life*. When I think of it in those terms, I would be willing to endure it all over again.

I know some people who read this book may be just like I used to be, trying to convince themselves that they have time to change. If that's you, I have one thing to tell you: *don't wait!* Don't make the mistake that I almost made. It could cost you way more than you're actually willing to pay. We serve an amazing God, one who forgives us when we really don't deserve it, even allowing us to start all over again if we need to, *and all we have to do is just ask.*

Even after ignoring God for all those years, when I reached out to Him in my darkest hour, He was there for me with His love, His acceptance, and a beautiful plan for my life. I don't pretend to fully understand why God has done for me all that He's done, why He decided to bless me with a recovery that was nothing short of a miracle. But one thing I do know is that I will spend the rest of my life demonstrating to Him and others that He made a good decision. I pray that every person reading this book can do the same.

May God bless you.

Now get up and stand on your feet. I have appeared to you to appoint you as a servant and as a witness of what you have seen of me and what I will show you (Acts 26:16).

About the Author

G.L. Woods was a man who had it all: a beautiful family, a successful career, and the ability to enjoy his passion for motocross. But all of that changed when, in 2004, he suffered an injury to his spinal cord that left him paralyzed from the neck down.

Today, G.L. Woods is an author and speaker who frequently shares his message of hope at churches, schools, conferences, and universities, as he tells his audiences about a God who still performs miracles—even when we may not deserve it.

G.L. and his wife, Tina, live with their two children, Bailey and Bryce, in Morgantown, Indiana. He has been a representative for Ozark National Life Insurance since 1986, and serves as an elder and children's Sunday school teacher at his home church, First Christian Church of Morgantown.

Contact the Author
To contact G.L. or to schedule him to speak to your group, go to:
www.glwoods.com
